Data-driven
Graphic Design

Fairchild Books
An imprint of Bloomsbury Publishing Plc
Imprint previously known as AVA Publishing

50 Bedford Square   1385 Broadway
London   New York
WC1B 3DP   NY 10018
UK   USA

www.bloomsbury.com

**FAIRCHILD BOOKS, BLOOMSBURY and the Diana logo are
trademarks of Bloomsbury Publishing Plc**

© Bloomsbury Publishing Plc, 2016

British Library Cataloguing-in-Publication Data
A catalogue record for this book is available from the British Library.
ISBN: PB: 978-1-4725-7830-3
        ePDF: 978-1-4725-7831-0

Library of Congress Cataloging-in-Publication Data
Richardson, Andrew (Lecturer in Design)
Data-driven graphic design: creative coding for visual communication / Andrew Richardson
      pages cm
Includes index.
ISBN 978-1-4725-7830-3 (pbk.) – ISBN 978-1-4725-7831-0 (epdf) –
1. Graphic arts–Data processing. 2. Computer programming. 1. Title.
T385.R4966 2016
006.6—dc23
        2015008891

Series: Required Reading Range, 1234567X

Typeset by Jane Harper
Printed and bound in China

Data-driven
Graphic Design
Creative Coding for
Visual Communication

Andrew Richardson

Fairchild Books
An imprint of Bloomsbury Publishing Plc

BLOOMSBURY
LONDON · OXFORD · NEW YORK · NEW DELHI · SYDNEY

CONTENTS

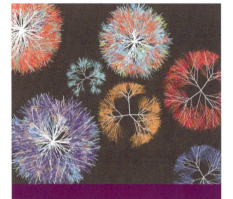

INTRODUCTION

Digital technology has become an increasingly important part of creative design and visual communication practice. As the tools and the technology for design change, grow and develop, so the number of opportunities for creative activity increase. In this growing technological environment, it is important that creative artists and designers play an active role in learning how to think about, approach, and use digital technology in order to harness its unique capabilities and characteristics, and push the boundaries of visual expression.

Rather than use these tools and environments "blindly" or unthinkingly, a critical and creative approach is needed which helps to develop new modes of visual expression and types of visual communication. By approaching digital environment in this open-minded way, everything is "up for grabs," there are no pre-defined or prescriptive outcomes, only possibilities: new modes of visual expression to be found and explored. Key to this way of thinking is a creative approach to, and understanding of, the computer as a visually data-driven design tool.

At its heart, the computer is an amazing data "input and output" device; able to pull in huge amounts and types of information, images, colors, numbers, words, sounds etc. from a wide range of input sources (user interaction, file sharing, online connection etc.), outputting them to the screen as graphics, images, or animations. When coupled with its amazing processing capability, the input-output data flow of the computer makes it a unique

"design environment" capable of creating new types of dynamically generated visuals. Dynamic shapes and forms can be generated which can be used within a wide range of visual and graphic design contexts. Using and understanding the technology, being able to think about the uniqueness of the computer environment, its possibilities and capabilities, opens up a great many creative opportunities to create pieces of work which visually embody the dynamic, flexible, and adaptable characteristics of the digital environment.

An important part of harnessing the processing ability of the computer is programming code. Code is at the heart of the input/output digital world, it is the way through which data is transmitted, translated and transformed from an ("input") stream of information and output as a variety of static and moving visual forms. Understanding and using code as part of a broader approach to creative digital practice allows designers to engage with the wider potential of the computer as a data-driven device. Even a small understanding of the concepts of the way programming code gets and processes data expands the horizons for creative design solutions and allows a broader range of design outcomes and possibilities to be considered.

Written as an inspiring overview of the intersections between visual communication and code, this book provides an introduction to the ways in which a broad approach to the computer as a data input /output device has been used to create new, uniquely "data-driven" visuals, inspiring experimental approaches to "traditional" areas of graphic design. Starting with the basic concepts, each chapter outlines how different types of data "input" (e.g. numbers, text, images etc.) can be harnessed, via code, to generate innovative types of output, i.e. creative visual outcomes both for print and screen. Examples of design and art pieces, provide creative context and inspiration, whilst more detailed (step-by-step) guides to the techniques of writing programming code, situated at the end of each chapter, provide the introduction to basic practical tools to enable a fresh approach to designing with and for the data-driven environment.

The book can be used as an overview of concepts, a source of visual and creative inspiration, or as a starting point for learning the fundamental elements of code. Hopefully it will be a text which you will return to at different points of your own creative process. Whether or not you become a programmer, the ideas and examples in the book will remain relevant even as the technology changes.

This vast and interesting subject can lead off in many different creative directions. As the examples of work and the designers in this book illustrate, a lot of new and exciting things happen by playing with code. Hopefully this represents just the first step on a long and exciting creative journey: An open mind, a healthy dose of curiosity, a desire to explore new things and a willingness to make, and learn from, mistakes will take you a long way. Good luck.

CHAPTER ONE
DESIGNERS AND CODE

1

"Try to get the most out of your material,
but always in such a way as honors it most."
William Morris

THE COMPUTER AS A CREATIVE ENVIRONMENT

"Reactive" Graphics

The introduction of computer processes has shifted the everyday tools and methods of the graphic design process from the physical environment of ink and paper to the digital environment of pixels and screens. Designers are now able to edit, copy, enhance, manipulate, transform, and combine visuals in ways not imaginable using traditional processes. The computer is, however, much more than just a digital canvas, darkroom, or editing suite. By looking beyond the confines of the software tools, it is possible to see the computer as a creative medium in its own right, with its own unique set of properties, characteristics, and attributes that open up new possibilities for creative practice. Just as physical materials, paper, ink, and paint each have their own individual qualities to be considered and manipulated, so too the computer has its own unique abilities and characteristics to be creatively explored. Seeing and using the built-in potential of the computer as a device that can take and use lots of different types of data input (e.g., from mouse, video camera, or microphone) to generate visuals opens up new ways of thinking, new ways of working, and new types of computationally created images.

Computers are fantastic data processing and calculation devices, designed for manipulating and processing huge amounts of information immensely quickly. The ability of the computer to take, use, and combine media means that it can connect visuals and data quickly and in interesting ways. Information input via connected data sources (web files, sounds, video, or text) can be used to generate a wide range of digital images, objects, or environments. The enormous processing capability of the computer to use and transform media (images, text, video, or sound) in a "live" or interactive format forms a great source of creative innovation and possibility. A digital sound source can, for example, be used to generate a drawing; a piece of text can be visually translated into a graphical image; the data from the movement of people passing in front of a shop window can be used to create projected images and sounds. Visuals created in this way move beyond traditional graphics and become new kinds of reactive, interactive, or "generative" graphics created in response to data input. These kinds of graphics are unique, responsive to their environment, and only possible by harnessing the processing ability of the computer. Exploring the possibilities of the computer as a device for generating reactive graphics therefore opens up new possibilities for re-thinking digital objects and exceeding the boundaries of traditional image editing and digital graphics software.

THE COMPUTER
AS A CREATIVE
ENVIRONMENT

CODE:
MANIPULATING
THE MEDIUM

GETTING
STARTED

CODE:
VOCABULARY
AND
INSTRUCTIONS

1.2

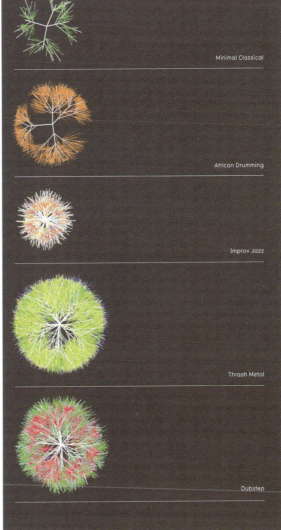

Minimal Classical

African Drumming

Improv Jazz

Thrash Metal

Dubstep

1.2 Seconde Nature, Universal Everything

An audio-reactive identity generator for a music venue in Aix-En-Provence, France. Computer reactive trees grow in response to being played different genres of music. Vector files are produced for use by the venue's communications team.

CODE: MANIPULATING THE MEDIUM

Code and Creativity

Exploring the creative potential of the computer as a data processing machine means creating bespoke programs (software) to manipulate and sort digital information (text, images, etc.), using and transforming it to create new visual outcomes. In the physical environment, human hands manipulate materials, such as pen on paper or paint on canvas. In the computational environment, data is directly manipulated into digital objects by writing lines of programming code.

Every object that exists in the digital environment is created and controlled by code. Every digital tool that you use (word processor, image editor, web browser) is created using programming code. When you are writing a book, sending an email, or editing a photograph, behind the glossy drag-and-drop menus and user interfaces, the computer is busy processing the programming instructions to perform the necessary tasks. Code can be used for a range of tasks and purposes; it can be used to create a single web page or to create large-scale software applications. Using code provides a natural and direct way of making and manipulating the digital environment.

Programming languages come in many different forms and are used in lots of different contexts. Each language is created for a specific purpose, created to work with a specific set of media or perform a specific set of tasks. Each programming language has its own vocabulary and grammar, which define the range and scope of the language and determine the type of tasks that it can perform. Common languages include Java, JavaScript, and C#. Just as learning a new foreign language allows the speaker to connect with new people and opens up opportunities for communication, so too learning a programming language allows the programmer to communicate directly with the computer and opens up new opportunities for creating digital objects and environments.

Like natural languages, programming languages have vocabularies and grammars. Unlike natural languages, the words of a programming language are often limited to instructions and commands, and the rules of usage are strict and well defined. Instructions have to be written precisely; otherwise, the computer does not know what to do and the program will not work. There is little scope to be descriptive with a programming language—no poetry, just commands.

All designers, whatever their medium, need to have an appreciation for and understanding of their material. Experience of the processes, characteristics, limitations and abilities of their media plays a crucial part in creating a successful and practical design solution, which makes the best and most appropriate use of the materials. Artists and designers keen to explore the qualities, characteristics and creative possibilities of the computer environment do so using code; just as print-based designers who have an understanding of paper-weights, print processes, color separations, etc., use this experience to inform their design work, so, designers working towards screen-based outcomes who have understanding of code can use this knowledge to develop design informed, creative design solutions. Understanding the way code works opens up new ways of thinking about and designing with and for the digital environment; it presents fresh opportunities for creative thought, and provides opportunities to design amazing digital visuals and experiences.

THE COMPUTER
AS A CREATIVE
ENVIRONMENT

CODE:
MANIPULATING
THE MEDIUM

GETTING
STARTED

CODE:
VOCABULARY
AND
INSTRUCTIONS

1.3

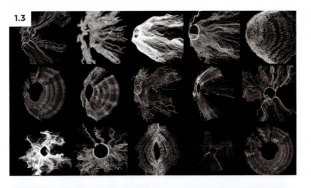

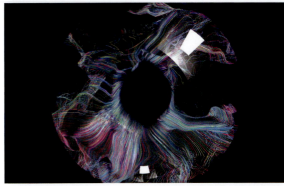

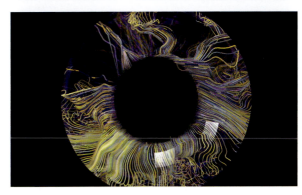

1.3 Big Eyes, Identity Illustrations, FIELD and SomeOne
An example of design work which makes innovative use of data-driven processes. The system created for an ad agency is based on generative digital images resembling the human iris. The visuals are adaptive, flexible, and data-powered, which change depending on their context and application, creating unique designs for each application. The eyes can mirror visiting clients and can be activated by client data, big or small. The flexible element of the visual brand identity creates a flexible cohesive visual approach that can be applied across lots of different types of media.

Code is a useful and powerful creative tool that artists and designers use to explore the creative possibilities of the digital environment and to create original digital objects, designs, and artworks. By writing code, designers can create interactive games, generate visuals that respond to user input or the physical environment, draw generative graphics, or manipulate typography. Writing code opens up new opportunities to create unique, individual digital objects and environments as well as application and system software.

Programming is a creative process unlike any other; it is a flexible and "natural" way of engaging with and harnessing the digital processing power of the computer for creative visual output. It provides new possibilities to create objects and solutions that would be otherwise un-thinkable. Rather than limiting themselves to digital drawing and editing tools, artists and designers can use code to create and invent their own drawing tools and applications.

EXEMPLAR

John Maeda

John Maeda is a graphic designer and computer scientist who has been a highly influential voice in the area of design and technology with a particular interest in the way that these areas merge and intersect. As a designer, Maeda's early work combined computer code with design aesthetics—a combination that redefined the use of code as a tool for visual expression, and paved the way for future generations of interactive media designers.

1.4

1.4 *Design by Numbers*
John Maeda
The graphic design work of John Maeda combines a uniquely Japanese aesthetic with computational processes that result in characteristically elegant pieces of design both for print and screen.

THE COMPUTER
AS A CREATIVE
ENVIRONMENT

**CODE:
MANIPULATING
THE MEDIUM**

GETTING
STARTED

CODE:
VOCABULARY
AND
INSTRUCTIONS

Design by Numbers (DBN)

Design By Numbers (DBN) was a programming language and environment created by John Maeda in 1999 as part of his Aesthetics and Computation Group to teach coding to designers and artists. The goals of the project were to introduce code as a way to think about creating design for the screen and to provide a useful tool for introducing code to a visually literate community. The language provided a unified interface for writing and running simple programs. Using a minimal screen grid of 100 by 100 pixels and a limited set of commands and functions, the programming environment distilled the basic structures, concepts, and commands of computation, encouraging the designer to think carefully about designing within these constraints.

The associated DBN book is beautiful, and it is as much a discussion of the concepts of code as it is an instruction manual for the language. Although the programming language itself is no longer in use, the project proved to be highly influential; its legacy continues to be felt. DBN had a huge influence on the subsequent development of the Processing programming language created by two of Maeda's students, Ben Fry and Casey Reas. Fry and Reas developed Processing in order to continue the original idea of DBN: creating a programming environment for designers.

Reactive Square (Reactive Books)

John Maeda's early interest in the use of computer code as a design material—one that can be used as creatively as a brush or a pen—has inspired and influenced a generation of digital designers. His work and his writing established the idea that code could be used to create new types of visual design. He laid the foundations for an area of design that is now often referred to as "creative coding."

His early experiments in the creative and visual applications of computer programming may look simple now, but they were (and still are) unique pieces of digital design that prepared the ground for many of the interactive graphics we see today. His idea of "reactive graphics," used to describe visual shapes and type that move and respond to specific types of computer and user input, still resonates.

1.5

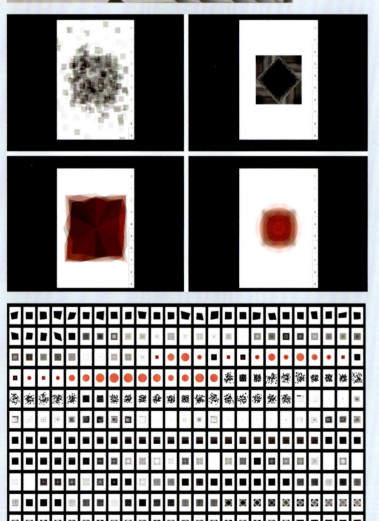

1.5 *Reactive Square Series*
John Maeda
Maeda's "Reactive Square" Series were important early experiments exploring the visual possibilities of the computer as an environment for creating new types of design. Looking beyond the limitations of software Maeda explored the computer as a creative medium which could create graphics responsive to user input, such as sound.

THE COMPUTER
AS A CREATIVE
ENVIRONMENT

**CODE:
MANIPULATING
THE MEDIUM**

GETTING
STARTED

CODE:
VOCABULARY
AND
INSTRUCTIONS

Between 1994 and 1999, Maeda created a series of digital books to explore and develop the notion of "reactive graphics." Each book explored a single type of input source to generate the graphics: microphone, mouse, time, and keyboard. The first book was *The Reactive Square*: ten squares that respond to audio from the microphone. The second was *Flying Letters*, which used the mouse as a way of playing with digital type forms. The third was twelve playful clocks called "12 o'clocks" that displayed the time in a specific digital format. The final book, *Tap, Type, Write*, was a digital interaction inspired by the typewriter; it used the keyboard as input. The single input source used for each book of experiments, together with the visual simplicity and playfulness of each piece, created a series of compelling pieces of work which introduced a new way of looking at and thinking about digital design for a new generation of artists and designers. These books are now hard to view because they require a Mac with pre-OS X software, but their ideas and concepts remain as vivid as ever.

1.6

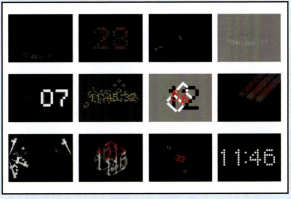

1.6 *12 o'clocks* **John Maeda**
Each of the "reactive books" was a playful experiment in digital aesthetics presented as a book-based CD-ROM. The 1996 typographic project of the 12 o'clocks, seen here, was an early forerunner to the interactive media that has since seen explosive growth.

GETTING STARTED

One of the attractions of exploring code is its accessibility. Unlike buying the latest version of design software, getting started with a programming language does not require any huge financial outlay. As long as you have access to an Internet-connected computer, you can download and access resources for free and immediately start experimenting and exploring the processes and ideas of the language.

Most programming languages are created and delivered as "open source" projects, which means that they are free for use and development. A large and growing open source community of designers, programmers, artists, experts, and novices alike share ideas, projects, source code, and resources for expanding the capability of each language. When starting to explore the creative possibilities of code, the main requirements to begin your journey are a healthy dose of curiosity (a desire to understand how things work and to look under the "hood" of the computer), an interest in experimenting with new ideas, and a willingness to make mistakes.

Tools and technology

There are lots of different programming languages and environments available for designers to use. Each language and environment has specific strengths that make it appropriate to a particular type of work (e.g., dealing with video, online data, etc.). The following is a brief overview of some of the most commonly used programming environments used by creative coders, artists, and designers.

Processing: www.processing.org

Processing is a programming language created to give artists and designers a simple way to create interactive drawings and graphics and to teach the fundamentals of programming code. Initially created as a tool to teach software literacy to the visual art and design community, the program has evolved into a language that is used by students and professionals alike. The Processing environment is a "ring fenced" version of the (much larger) Java language; it allows users to quickly get into creating code-generated visuals. Code is written as "sketches" that can be quickly and easily tested. Over the years, the language and the community have grown such that it is now a full-blown design and prototyping tool used for large-scale installation work, motion graphics, and data visualizations. Processing will be used as the programming environment for the examples and tutorials used in this book.

VVVV: vvvv.org

VVVV (also called "v4" or "v-four") is a programming environment with a particular emphasis on real-time video work, and it is used for creating large-scale media environments with physical interfaces and real-time motion graphics, audio, and video. Although it is a programming environment, VVVV uses a graphical programming tool editor that allows interactions and environments to be created visually, without having to write lines of programming code as text. Individual instructions and functions are represented as boxes (nodes), which the user links together to pass data between them. An entire structure composed of nodes and links is called a "patch." Although VVVV provides a visual way of representing the structure of a program, the interface is not intuitive, and complex programs can quickly create an intricate web of nodes and links.

openFrameworks: www.openframeworks.cc

OpenFrameworks is a software library designed for creative coding. It has been created to allow designers and artists to make pieces that combine media elements (graphics, sound, video, etc.) in an interactive way. The idea behind openFrameworks is very similar to that of Processing. However, unlike Processing, openFrameworks is not a programming language; it is a toolkit, a "glue" that brings together lots of different programming libraries and assets into a single framework. This makes openFrameworks more flexible and powerful, especially when creating 3D graphics and real-time manipulation of video. The library structure and framework does, however, make it sometimes confusing or difficult for novice programmers to navigate.

THE COMPUTER
AS A CREATIVE
ENVIRONMENT

CODE:
MANIPULATING
THE MEDIUM

**GETTING
STARTED**

CODE:
VOCABULARY
AND
INSTRUCTIONS

1.7

1.7 Processing
A screen shot from the
Processing development
environment. Code is written
directly into the text editor.
The display window shows the
results of the code when it is
run.

1.8

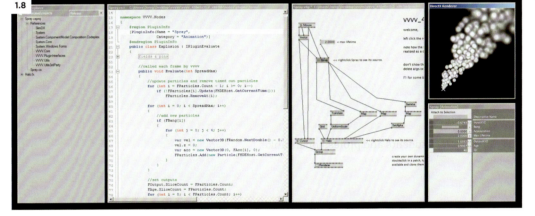

1.8 VVVV
A screen-shot from VVVV, which
uses a hybrid visual and textual
development environment.

NodeBox3: www.nodebox.net/node/
NodeBox 3 is a visual programming tool that is designed for creating data visualizations quickly and easily. Programs in NodeBox 3 are constructed visually by dragging boxes (nodes) onto the screen and linking them together. Each node performs a specific task (function), the details of which can be edited by selecting from menu items within each node. External data can be plugged into the nodes to set and change the on-screen visuals. The ability to visually construct programs by linking boxes together makes it an interesting starting point for the beginner. Although individual nodes can be custom built and edited using Python, the programming environment is not as wide ranging and "expressive" as some of the other examples. The trade-off for the visual interface is that there is less flexibility and control. It is a good tool to explore for experimenting with data visualizations. A new version, NodeBox Live, runs in the browser and will support both visual programming (through nodes) and textual programming (using JavaScript).

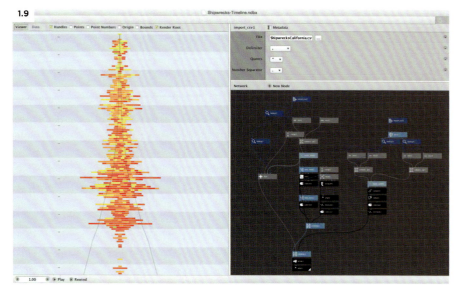

1.9 *NodeBox 3* **J. Aulbach, 2012**
Visualization of shipwrecks of California.

HTML, CSS, and JavaScript
In addition to these creative code environments, there are other mainstream programming languages and scripts that are used on the web. HTML and CSS are specific "mark up" languages used to create the content and look of a webpage. JavaScript is a programming language used to create interactivity and games on the web. Although this book will not specifically look at JavaScript, the core principles of programming used in many of these examples are shared across many languages, including JavaScript.

THE COMPUTER
AS A CREATIVE
ENVIRONMENT

CODE:
MANIPULATING
THE MEDIUM

GETTING
STARTED

CODE:
VOCABULARY
AND
INSTRUCTIONS

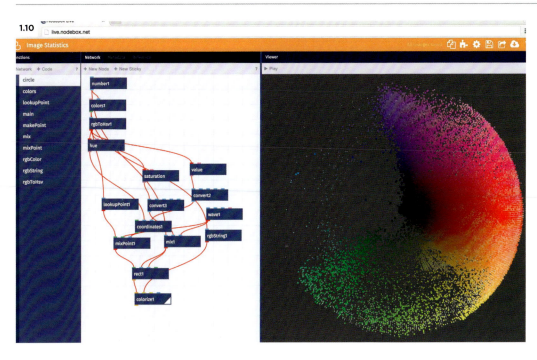

1.10 *NodeBox Live* **F. De Bleser, 2014**
Image visualized as a color circle.

Code is not only used as an individual stand-alone language; it can also be used within a piece of software to enhance or add functionality or introduce elements of interactivity. This can be done to save time and automate repetitive processes or to generate work dynamically. For example, the popular motion graphics software, Adobe After Effects, has its own built-in programming environment called Expressions that can be used to create dynamic animations without manually adding many key frames. The Expressions scripts are based on the language system and structure of JavaScript. Similarly, the animation tool Adobe Flash has its own built-in programming language called actionScript. ActionScript has evolved with the software; it has grown from a simple set of functions into a language capable of adding a wide range of levels of interaction and developed from simple button presses and menu items to fully dynamic animations generated entirely by code. The ability to add interaction to an animation using actionScript has made it a popular tool for designers, although it is now more commonly used for creating online games.

Processing
The examples in this book use Processing as the default language. Processing is a good all-round programming environment; it is freely available, easy to get up and running, and well supported with a large online community and plenty of example code. The Processing language uses programming concepts that are common to other languages and environments, so it provides a good starter language in which to learn the basic concepts of programming, which can be translated into other environments. Although the code examples given in the book are specifically built with Processing, most of the concepts are common to all programming structures, and so provide good overview of the fundamentals of code.

CODE: VOCABULARY AND INSTRUCTIONS

Work along with the examples in this section and, in addition, use the book resources available online. Get started with code by downloading the Processing development environment now! It is easy to install and ready to use from: https://processing.org/download/

The Processing website is home to a lively community of artists, designers, and programmers. It includes a host of useful guides and tutorials that will act as helpful references alongside the examples in this book.

This section will start by introducing some of the main elements of code that are common to many programming languages. They are very important and form the basic principles from which the rest of the examples in this book will be created.

Functions

Go to www.bloomsbury.com/richardson-data-driven, Chapter 1, and click on the project "Adding Color."

Every programming language consists of its own set of pre-written instructions, which tell the program what to do. These are called "functions," and they direct the code to perform specific tasks. Each programming language includes its own functions, which are usually listed in a reference guide. Functions are written by name, followed by a set of parentheses() and a semi-colon (;) to end the line.

```
doSomething();
```

In Processing, for example, a function to "smooth" the appearance of graphics on screen is:

```
// a function to draw graphics with an anti-aliased
edge
smooth();
```

The online Processing reference guide gives details of each function and indicates which (and how many) arguments any function requires. See https://processing.org/reference/

The brackets are used for extra information (called "arguments") to specify how the function works. For example, the function to set the width of a line includes a single argument, a number, to indicate a width in pixels:

```
// set the stroke to 10 pixels wide
strokeWeight(10);

// set the stroke to 5 pixels wide
strokeWeight(5);
```

Arguments can be displayed as numbers or as other types of data, such as text. The println() function, used to print text in the output window, specifies the text to display within the brackets.

```
// outputs the word "hello" to the output window
println("hello");
```

Functions often need more than one argument to work. Extra arguments are separated using a comma:

```
// sets the width and height of the screen size
size(200, 300);
```

Arguments of different data types can be used together. For example, the function for writing text on the screen needs to know what the text is as well as the numeric x, y location of the words:

```
text ("hello", 10, 20);
```

THE COMPUTER
AS A CREATIVE
ENVIRONMENT

CODE:
MANIPULATING
THE MEDIUM

GETTING
STARTED

CODE:
VOCABULARY
AND
INSTRUCTIONS

Functions have to be typed in exactly the correct way. Any mistakes in lowercase characters, uppercase characters, or spelling will cause the code to return an error message.

TRY IT

Create a new Processing sketch. Use the size() function to set the size of the window. Use the println() function to print a message in the "output" area.

Grammar and Syntax

Go to www.bloomsbury.com/richardson-data-driven, Chapter 1, and click on the project "Syntax Examples."

Just as written languages use punctuation (such as commas and periods) and paragraphs to structure a piece of writing and thus to help the reader understand its content, so programming languages also have their own set of punctuation marks used to structure a piece of code, which help the computer to read the instructions correctly.

The following is a short list of common grammatical elements used in programming to define the structure of code.

Semi-colon (;): This is a small but important part of code that is used to end a line, similar to the full stop of a period. Each command or instruction is ended with a semi-colon so that the computer knows where the end of a command is. Without these, several lines of code merge into one, creating errors.

```
// incorrect and will result in an error
size (200, 200)

size (200, 300); // correct
```

Curly brackets ({}): These indicate a "block" of code, similar to a paragraph. A large section of a program is often delineated as a single block of code. The curly brackets show where the block of code begins and ends. Brackets have to be paired; each opening bracket has to have a corresponding closing bracket.

```
{
    a line of code;
    Another line of code;
}
```

Blocks of code can be "nested" inside one another. Specific elements, such as "if statements," are structured using curly brackets.

Comments (//): These are the notes and annotations written in the code that are ignored by the computer. All programming languages include the ability to add comments, which can make the code more readable to yourself and others. In Processing, a comment is added into code using two forward slash symbols (//).

```
// this is a comment
smooth( );
// and this is a comment also
```

Many of the code examples in the book will include comments alongside the code to help explain it.

Variables

Go to www.bloomsbury.com/richardson-data-driven, Chapter 1, and click on the project "Variable Types."

Variables are at the heart of many programming concepts and provide the cornerstone for creating digitally dynamic, responsive graphics. A variable is simply a named container, which represents a piece of stored information. The name of the container remains the same, but the information it stores can be changed or retrieved while the program runs. Variables can be used for keeping track of information such as a player's game score, the location of an object on the screen, or the name of a user.

Variables are created, usually at the start of a program, by defining a name (without spaces) and data "type" (something that says what type of data is being stored). They are often given an initial (starting) value. Variables are usually named in a way that reflects how they will be used.

```
// creates a number variable called score
int score = 0;

// creates a number variable called x_pos
float x_pos = 120.5;

// creates a variable to store a user name
String userName = "Bill";
```

Once a variable has been created, it exists within the program and can be used elsewhere in the code in the place of fixed data values.

```
String name = "Andrew"; // creates a variable
// prints out the variable name ("Andrew")
println (name);
float thickness = 10;
strokeWeight (thickness);
```

The value (the content) of a variable can be updated and changed while the program runs.

```
String name = "Bill";
println (name); // prints "Bill"
name = "Bob";
println (name); // prints "Bob"
```

Number variables can be altered mathematically or via other input, such as user interaction (e.g., mouse movement).

Simple mathematical calculations are often used to "increment" (increase) or "decrement" (decrease) numeric variables.

```
float xpos = 100;
xpos = xpos + 10; // increase by 10 (to 110)
xpos = xpos - 20; // decrease by 20 (to 90)
// scale (multiply) by 10 (to 900)
xpos = xpos * 10;
xpos = xpos / 2; // divide by 2 (to 450)
```

In programming languages the basic mathematical symbols are:

```
Addition: +
Subtraction: -
Multiplication: *
Division: /
```

The following is "shorthand" way of writing the same calculations:

```
xpos += 10;
xpos -= 20;
xpos *= 10;
xpos /= 2;
```

Changing number variables are often used in drawing functions, which set the location of a shape drawn on the screen. Updating the variable therefore changes the location and moves the shape.

Variable Data Types

Variables can be used to store lots of different kinds of data, (numbers, text, colors). When a variable is created it is assigned a "data type" to define the "type" of information it is going to store. The data type is written before the variable name when it is created:

```
int x = 10; // a variable with an "int" data type
```

The basic data types (which will be used in this text) are as follows:

Integer (int): The int data type is used for storing whole numbers (integers), commonly used for values that will always be a whole number (e.g., a player's score in a game).

```
int score = 50;
```

Float: A float value is also a number, but it is able to store decimal, or "floating number," values. These are commonly used for values that may need to be precisely defined or changed—for example, when calculating a changing angle or movement of an object across the screen.

```
float angle = 45.5;
```

THE COMPUTER
AS A CREATIVE
ENVIRONMENT

CODE:
MANIPULATING
THE MEDIUM

GETTING
STARTED

**CODE:
VOCABULARY
AND
INSTRUCTIONS**

String: A String is a piece of data that stores a sequence (a "string") of characters, often letters, inside speech marks. Strings are commonly used for saving literal text, such as user names.

```
String name = "Andrew";
```

Boolean: Boolean data types are those that can have a value of either true or false. They are useful for creating objects that can be used as a type of "switch" in the code that can be turned either "on" or "off." These values are often used in conditional statements (see below) to determine the flow of a program.

```
Boolean visible = true;
```

TRY IT

Try creating your own variable (String, int, or float).
Give it a name, a data type, and a starting value.
Put the variable inside the println() function to output its value.
Update or change the variable value to see how this changes the messages that are printed.

Making Decisions

Go to www.bloomsbury.com/richardson-data-driven, Chapter 1, and click on the project "If Statements."

Controlling the "flow" of a program is at the heart of any interactive or generative process. It allows the outcomes of the program to change according to a range of conditions and prevents the program from producing the same results every time it is run.

If Statements

"If" statements are common to many programming languages. Also known as "conditional statements," the basic concept is simple; a block of code is created that will be run only if a condition is true. The structure of an "if" statement is as follows:

```
if (condition) {
    do this if condition is true;
}
```

The condition to be tested is written inside the parentheses. If it is true, then the instructions inside the curly braces are executed; if not, then they are simply ignored.

The following statement checks to see if a Boolean value of a variable ("visible") is true and, if it is, provides instructions to show some graphics.

```
if (visible == true) {
    // show graphics;
}
```

"If" statements can be also be used to check the value of a number and compare it with another. Standard mathematical symbols are used to assess whether a number is greater than (>), less than (<), or equal to (==) another. The following examples are used to check if a player's score is below 20 or above 50 and outputs a message accordingly.

Mathematical conditions used in "if" statements:

```
Greater Than: >
Less Than: <
Equal To: ==
Greater Than or Equal to: >=
Less Than or Equal to: <=
```

```
if (score < 20) {
   println ("bad luck");
}

 if (score > 50) {
   println ("well done");
}
```

"If" statements can also include a extra part to determine what happens if the initial condition is not met. In other words, "if this is true" then do something; otherwise, ("if it is not true") do something else. Adding the "else" statement creates two different outcomes. In the following statement one of two statements are printed out, according to whether or not the value of "age" is greater than 60:

```
if (age > 60) {
   println ("you are over 60");
} else {
   println ("you are 60 or under");
}
```

TRY IT

Create a numeric variable called "score," and give it an initial value. Write an "if" statement that prints out a message if the value of "score" is less than 50. Add other "if" statements to print different messages depending on the value of "score."

Loops

Go to www.bloomsbury.com/richardson-data-driven, Chapter 1, and click on the project "For Loops."

Looped elements in a program provide a very quick and useful way of counting, by working through lists, and for creating structured, ordered sequences. A common type of loop used in programming is a "for" loop. "For" loops use a variable "counter" and comprise three elements: the starting value of the variable; a test condition, which is checked to see whether to remain in or exit the loop; and an "update" statement, which changes the variable at the end of each loop (usually increasing it by one).

The following standard "for" loop creates a variable (i), which starts at zero (int i=0), loops while i is less than 10 (i<10), and increases i by one at the end of each loop (i++).

```
for (int i=0; i<10; i++) {
   println (i); // outputs "0 1 2 3 4 5 6 7 8 9"
}
```

Each iteration of the loop calls the println instruction, which outputs the value of the variable. The println() function is repeated 10 times, outputting the value of "i" each time, generating a number sequence 0 to 9.

TRY IT

Create a "for" loop to count values from 0 to 9.
Alter the number that the loop counts up to by changing the value in the "i<10" element of the loop.

THE COMPUTER
AS A CREATIVE
ENVIRONMENT

CODE:
MANIPULATING
THE MEDIUM

GETTING
STARTED

**CODE:
VOCABULARY
AND
INSTRUCTIONS**

User-defined Functions

*Go to www.bloomsbury.com/richardson-data-driven,
Chapter 1, and click on the project "User Defined Functions."*

Programmers can go beyond the pre-written, built-in
functions, such as smooth() and println(), available in a
programming language to create additional functions,
which are re-usable blocks of code. A function is a
named wrapper for a group of instructions. Once created,
calling the name of the function automatically runs the
instructions. Wrapping instructions into a function makes
the code more useable and repeatable.

Creating a basic function is simple. Create a function by
giving it a name; a "return type" (the default is "void"); a
set of parentheses, into which variables can be added; and
a set of curly brackets, between which the instructions are
written. For example:

```
void myFunction ( ) {
  // do something
}
```

In this example, a function, called calcValue(), calculates
and prints the squared value of a number.

```
void calcValue() {
    float number = 3;
    println (number * number); // outputs 9
}
```

Once created, a function can be used like using any other
pre-written code instruction: by calling its name followed
by parentheses. Each time calcValue() is called, it performs
the calculation within the function and prints the value of
the sum.

```
calcValue(); // calls the function
```

Just as pre-built functions often use values (arguments)
to make them work, so user-defined functions can also
include variables to make them more useful.

A more practical version of the example function, previously,
would be to calculate and print the squared value of any given
number. To achieve this, a variable (num) is added between
the parentheses and used within the function to affect the
calculation.

```
void calcValue (float num) {
    float number = num;
    println (number * number);
}
```

The value of "num" is set when the function is called.

A single argument, a number, is put between the parentheses
to set the value of "num" and produce new results each time:

```
calcValue (4); // num=4, prints "16"
calcValue (12); // num=12, prints "144"
```

Additional arguments can be added to the function, which
have to be defined when it is called:

```
// a function now takes 2 number values (num1, num2)
void calcValue (float num1, float num2) {
    float number1 = num1;
    float number2 = num2;
    println (number1 * number2);
}

// when the function is called num1 and num2 are
multiplied together
calcValue (10, 2); // prints 20
calcValue (12, 5); // prints 60
```

If a function is called with misplaced or missing arguments,
it will return an error:

```
// wrong number of arguments (missing one)
calcValue (10);
// right number of arguments, wrong type
calcValue ("three," 2);
```

Functions are a really valuable part of code; they create a
useful way to create reusable elements in a program.

Loops in the Structure: setup() and draw()

Programming environments generally have two main structural blocks that define how and when the instructions are processed. The first creates the starting conditions for the program, a place which "initializes" the program so that everything is set up correctly as the program begins. The second defines what happens while the program is running: the looping part of the program in which instructions are repeatedly executed and processed. These blocks of code, the initializing function and the looping function, may have different names in different languages; in Processing, they are referred to as "setup()" and "draw()."

The setup() function is called once when the program starts. It is used to define initial properties, such as screen size. Code inside setup() is called only once.

```
void setup () {
    //code in here is run only once
}
```

The draw() function continually loops while the program is running. Any instructions or lines of code inside the draw function are continually repeated.

```
void draw() {
    //code in here is repeated
}
```

The setup() and draw() functions will be used as the basic structure for the examples used throughout the book.

Lists and Arrays

Go to www.bloomsbury.com/richardson-data-driven, Chapter 1, and click on the project "Arrays."

An array is a list of data, like a shopping list, commonly used by programming languages and useful for storing lots of variable values, such as number values (int, float) or text data (String).

An array is created by defining the type of data to store and the number of elements that can be added to the list. The following example creates a list called shoppingList, which has 4 elements, or "spaces," that can hold text data (String):

```
String [] shoppingList = new String [4];
```

The square brackets here are used when creating and accessing an array.

Once created, the array list is "populated" by putting data values to each element (each space) in the array. The square brackets are used to access items in the list. Elements in the array are numbered beginning at 0 (not 1). Data is assigned to the first item (element zero) in shoppingList as follows:

```
// the first item in the list is "apples"
shoppingList[0] = "apples";
```

The rest of the list can be populated in a similar way, using a number to refer to the position of the data in the list:

```
// the 2nd item in the shopping list
shoppingList[1] = "milk";

// the 3rd item in the shopping list
shoppingList[2] = "eggs";

// the 4th item in the shopping list
shoppingList[3] = "bread";
```

THE COMPUTER
AS A CREATIVE
ENVIRONMENT

CODE:
MANIPULATING
THE MEDIUM

GETTING
STARTED

**CODE:
VOCABULARY
AND
INSTRUCTIONS**

Once populated, items in an array can be found by referring to their element number (i.e., where they are in the list). Keep in mind that the first item is at element zero, so the last item in list of 4 items will be at element position 3.

```
println (shoppingList[0]); // prints out "apples"
println (shoppingList[1]); // prints out "milk"
println (shoppingList[2]); // prints out "eggs"
println (shoppingList[3]); // prints out "bread"
```

Each array has a variable called "length"; this is a number that returns the total number of elements in an array.

```
println (shoppingList.length); // prints out "4"
```

"For" loops provide a quick way of cycling through lists to access or change the data. A "for" loop works as a counter that can quickly access each of the array elements, one at a time. The following example cycles through and prints out each item in the shoppingList array. As the value of "i" changes within the "for" loop, so each element in the array is found in turn.

```
for (int i=0; i<shoppingList.length; i++) {
    // prints one element in the array, each time
    println (shoppingList[i]);
}
```

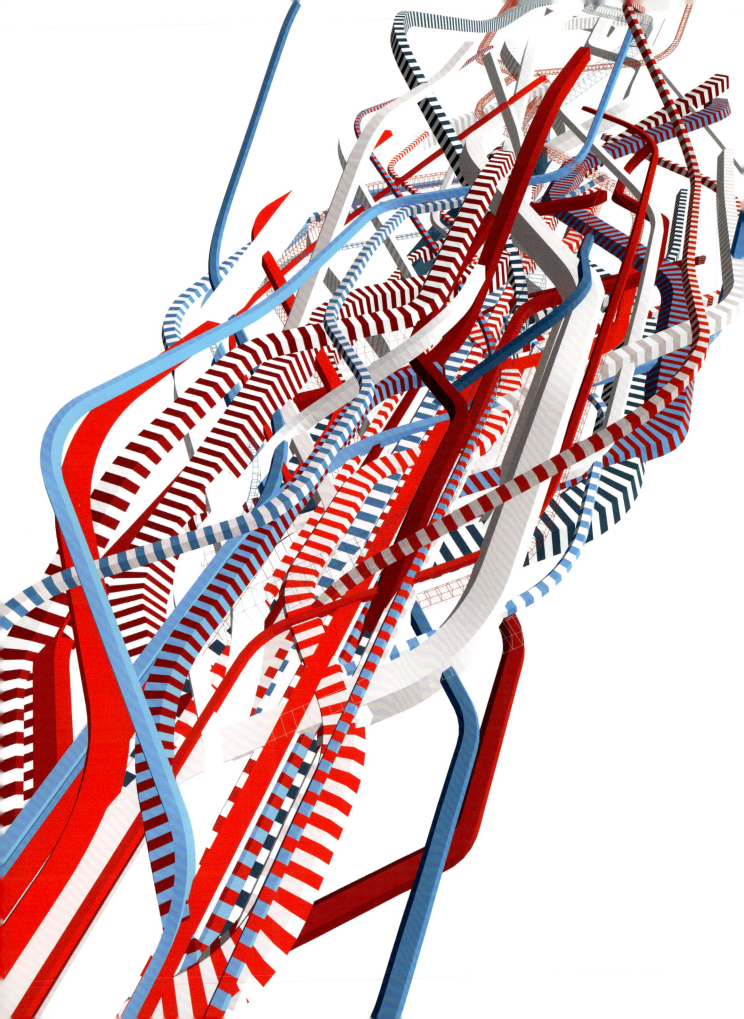

CHAPTER TWO
DRAWING WITH NUMBERS

"Everything is Number"

Pythagorus

DRAWING INSTRUCTIONS

Drawing using code provides designers with a unique set of opportunities and tools for creating digitally dynamic graphics; it is a process that requires a different approach to, and way of thinking about, how images are made, and it opens up new avenues for visual expression.

Unlike the physical process of making a mark with a pen, brush, or even a digital tablet, computational drawings are created by a written list of programming instructions based on rules and procedures that a programmer writes; a computer translates and executes the instructions into individual marks, lines, and shapes on the screen. Most programming languages include a set of specific instructions that generate simple geometric shapes (circles, squares, and lines) and that plot and position those shapes on the screen in a way that is similar to how we plot and draw shapes on a piece of graph paper. In the programming environment, these simple geometric forms are the most basic visual units from which the vast array of visually complex graphics can be generated. Although they are simple, when combined and repeated hundreds or even thousands of times within a program, these shapes can create new and more visually complex shapes. Learning how to use code to create the most basic shapes is an important first step towards developing complex data-driven graphics. Although a traditional drawing begins with a single mark on paper, a (dynamic) code-based drawing begins with writing an instruction to plot a line or dot on the screen.

See Code section: Drawing Shapes (page 56).

A significant part of the unique drawing power of code lies in its ability to harness the immense processing capacity of the computer. The way in which a computer can endlessly execute a series of drawing instructions over and over, hundreds of times per second, means that complex graphics and patterns can be generated from even just of a few lines of code. When combined and repeated, individual instructions act together as a kind of "drawing machine" that can generate a complex set of dense visuals. Added to this, the process usually includes elements that allow the program to generate individual varieties of shape and line based on internal or external data information fed into it. The programmer defines a generic set of drawing parameters; the computer then uses and interprets them to generate the visuals. The same set of programming instructions can, therefore, create a variety of unique and visually dense forms, graphics, and shapes that develop and change on the screen. Using the computer in this way establishes a creative "partnership" between the programmer and the computer that generates drawings and graphics that would be impossible using any traditional process.

Numbers and Number Sequences

Numbers are a key element within digital, screen-based graphics; they are fundamental to the way in which all digital images are understood and processed. Behind the gloss of the graphical user interface (GUI) of a digital painting or drawing program lies a hidden numeric environment that defines the details of the size, shape, position, color, and other features of every digital line and form drawn on the screen. We see this in practice every time software gives the user the ability to transform or define the details of a shape by entering number values that set its visual attributes, such as its width, height, rotation, location, or color. Adobe Illustrator, for example, allows users to see and set the size or position of a selected shape by altering number values in the Transform window.

Although largely hidden behind the GUI interface of the software, the importance and significance of numbers for creating digital graphics becomes unavoidable when programming. Individual number values are crucial to most aspects of the programming environment; they are the basic unit, the starting point, for all computational drawings, and they are used extensively in all pieces of code. Numbers are essential to define, describe, create, move, transform, and combine shapes, lines, animations, images, and words on screen. Every single programming function used to create even the simplest line or shape needs a set of numbers to define its exact position, size, shape, and even color.

DRAWING INSTRUCTIONS

NUMBER PATTERNS

REPETITION: SYSTEMATIC DRAWINGS

COMPLEXITY FROM SIMPLICITY

RANDOM DRAWINGS

DYNAMIC/ GENERATIVE DRAWINGS

CODE: DRAWING FUNCTIONS

2.2

2.2 2D SuperShapes. Reza Ali
2D SuperShapes is an application created by Reza Ali that allows users to play with numeric parameters to produce a range of organic shapes. Manipulation of the numbers creates an assortment of interesting and unexpected geometric forms.

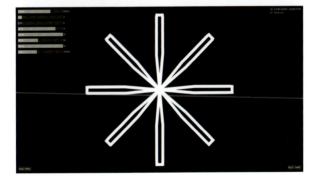

Using code to draw reveals what is happening behind the scenes of common graphical software such as Photoshop and Illustrator. By using programming code, artists and designers have the opportunity to dig "below the surface" of software; to directly "play" with the numerical data that is usually hidden to create, repeat, and combine shapes and graphics and this produce a wide variety of generative, data-driven, dynamic images.

The influence and use of number values is fundamentally important as a means of generating graphics and visuals. The direct connection between number values and visual properties available in the programming environment opens up a wide range of visual and conceptual possibilities for generating dynamic digital graphics. Number data can be sourced either from internal mathematical calculations or from external data sources and used to dynamically change the visual appearance of graphics (e.g., their shapes, sizes, colors, movements).

See Code section: Adding Variables (page 58).

NUMBER PATTERNS

The simplest way to create numbers to define visual output is by using numeric patterns created from a sequential, repetitive mathematical re-calculation of values. Number sequences can be used to create repeatable grids and other structures that provide visual order and harmony to a piece of art or design. They have inspired generations of artists and designers from a wide range of creative practices (e.g., art, music, and design) and have been applied to a variety of creative visual contexts—for example, the logical, functional visuals of Swiss modernist design; the geometric pattern of ornamental decoration; and the structure of a Philip Glass musical composition. The "mechanical" consistency and predictability of these values, when applied to a page, screen, or canvas, can create a clear sense of rhythm, balance, and harmony.

The repetitive re-positioning and combining of simple geometric shapes can, for example, be used to generate fabulously intricate patterns. Complex patterns emerge that contain a strong mathematical and visual rhythm harmony. The ornamentation found in Islamic pattern is a good example of numerically inspired repetitions of simple geometric shapes that create a wealth of highly decorative patterns.

In the programming environment, generating number sequences is a direct means of generating visuals. Simple mathematical calculations (e.g., increasing or decreasing a value) create sequences of numbers that can be applied to define any of the visual attributes of a shape (its size, movement, location, angle, color) and, therefore, used to generate rhythmic sequences of computationally generated pattern. The ability of the computer to process many hundreds of calculations very quickly, applying them to huge number of graphics, makes the repetition of numeric calculation something that can quickly yield complex visual patterns.

2.3 Islamic decorative art
Decorative tiles and designs used in Islamic art are typified by highly structured geometric patterns that are a representation of the spirituality of the Islamic world view and act as concrete symbols of the infinite. These types of geometric patterns have much in common with code-generated graphics. The natural ability of computer programming to infinitely repeat, redraw, scale, and change number values can generate a wide variety of geometrical patterns and shapes.

DRAWING
INSTRUCTIONS

NUMBER
PATTERNS

REPETITION:
SYSTEMATIC
DRAWINGS

COMPLEXITY
FROM SIMPLICITY

RANDOM
DRAWINGS

DYNAMIC/
GENERATIVE
DRAWINGS

CODE:
DRAWING
FUNCTIONS

2.3

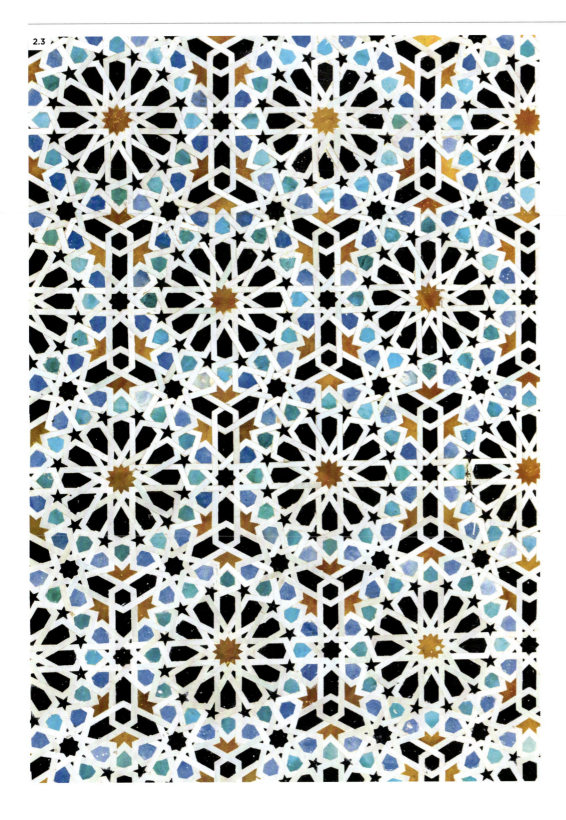

Once a link between a number pattern and visual attribute (e.g., rotation) has been created, any adjustments to its calculation, either intentional or accidental, will distort disrupt or change the visual outcome. A slight alteration to a calculation that, for example, is used to set the angle of a shape will alter or disrupt its rhythmically rotating pattern, creating a new version of shape and form. "Playing with" the number values—altering the way in which they are calculated and how they are applied—has a direct, and often surprising, effect on the final visual result. Simple number sequences can therefore generate repeatable shapes and patterns that can be used and re-used in many different ways.

2.4

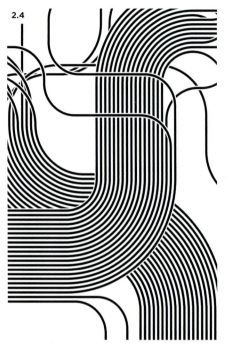

DRAWING
INSTRUCTIONS

NUMBER
PATTERNS

REPETITION:
SYSTEMATIC
DRAWINGS

COMPLEXITY
FROM SIMPLICITY

RANDOM
DRAWINGS

DYNAMIC/
GENERATIVE
DRAWINGS

CODE:
DRAWING
FUNCTIONS

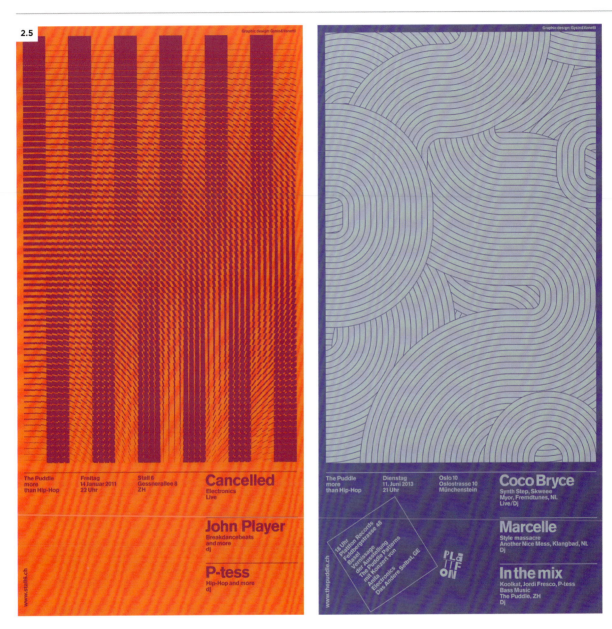

**2.4–2.5 Puddle Builder
Andreas Gysin and Sidi Vanetti**

Andreas Gysin and Sidi Vanetti used Processing to create a code-based drawing tool that generates a range of graphics that were ultimately used as promotional posters and flyers for the Puddle, a live electronic music event around Zürich. This project demonstrates how code can produce structured patterns and graphics from a numeric sequence.

EXEMPLAR

Marius Watz

Marius Watz is an artist whose work extensively explores the use of code-based and mathematical processes to generate striking computational images. The "algorithm," the code used to generate number patterns and sequences, is important to much of his work as he investigates ways of generating visually unique artifacts from code. The work is characterized by well-defined geometrical forms and vivid colors, and its range is extensive—from pure software works and projections to physical objects produced with digital fabrication technology.

2.6

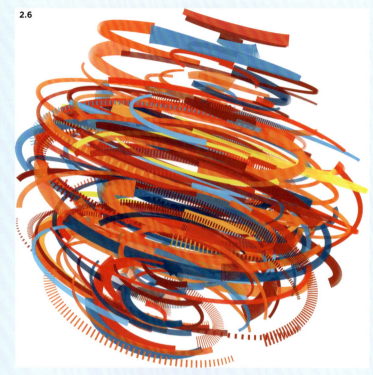

2.6 *Illuminations B*
Marius Watz
These images are taken from a sequence of 100 vector images that were generated by a specially written software system. A real-time projection of the images was used alongside the printed versions.

DRAWING
INSTRUCTIONS

NUMBER
PATTERNS

REPETITION:
SYSTEMATIC
DRAWINGS

COMPLEXITY
FROM SIMPLICITY

RANDOM
DRAWINGS

DYNAMIC/
GENERATIVE
DRAWINGS

CODE:
DRAWING
FUNCTIONS

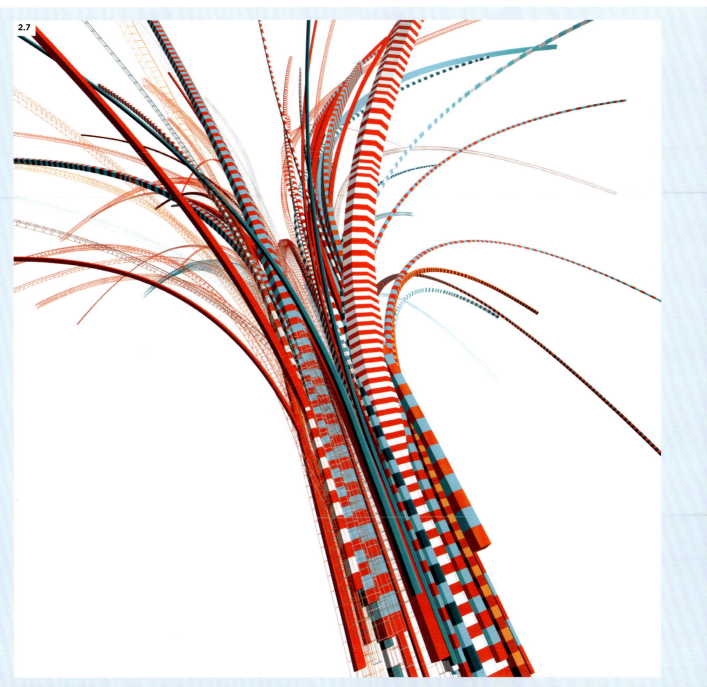

2.7 *Bridge Hypothesis*
Marius Watz
Still images taken from a
computationally generated
animation of geometric
forms that reflect the strong
structures of bridges and roads.
Watz designed the originals
to be viewed as a large-scale
projection.

REPETITION:
SYSTEMATIC DRAWINGS

Repetition is a concept at the heart of many digital design processes. Copy-and-paste or "step and repeat" procedures are common among many software drawing tools. They allow shapes to be repeatedly and accurately reproduced and transformed (scaled, rotated, moved, etc.) to create intricate repeating designs. The results of this type of process are organized and controlled, yet they produce variety. Repeatedly scaling and moving even a simple shape can create a kaleidoscopic array of shapes and patterns.

The idea of repetition is also a very important part of writing computer code. Code can quickly and accurately repeat an instruction or calculation or sort through a large set of data, and these key abilities are central to many of the tasks it is required to perform. Every programming language includes a range of different ways to loop (repeat) instructions or functions; they are part of the fabric, and structure of the programming environment. Built-in core functions—for example, draw()—are used to continually execute lines of code, repeatedly going over a list of instructions for as long as the program is running (potentially infinitely—or until the program is switched off).

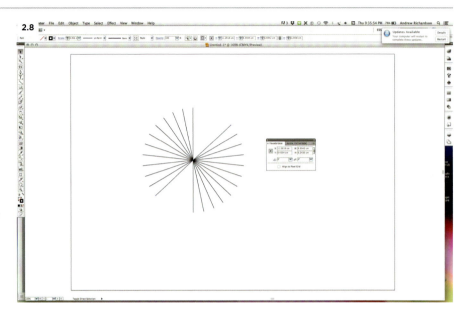

2.8

Other programming elements are specifically designed to loop (iterate) a series of instructions a set number of times; these kinds of loops (e.g., "for" loops or "while" loops) can be used to count through a list of items or alter and re-draw a shape a fixed number of times. Using looped (iterative) functions to generate a visual outcome creates graphics with a clear visual structure. A "for" loop function can be used, for example, to incrementally scale, move, or rotate a shape; it creates neat, regular, and well controlled visual results.

See Code Section: Repetition and Drawing with "For" Loops (page 59).

2.8 Illustrator screen shot
An example of the visual result from a "step and repeat" process in Adobe Illustrator, which can be used to generate simple geometric shapes and forms.

DRAWING
INSTRUCTIONS

NUMBER
PATTERNS

**REPETITION:
SYSTEMATIC
DRAWINGS**

COMPLEXITY
FROM SIMPLICITY

RANDOM
DRAWINGS

DYNAMIC/
GENERATIVE
DRAWINGS

CODE:
DRAWING
FUNCTIONS

2.9

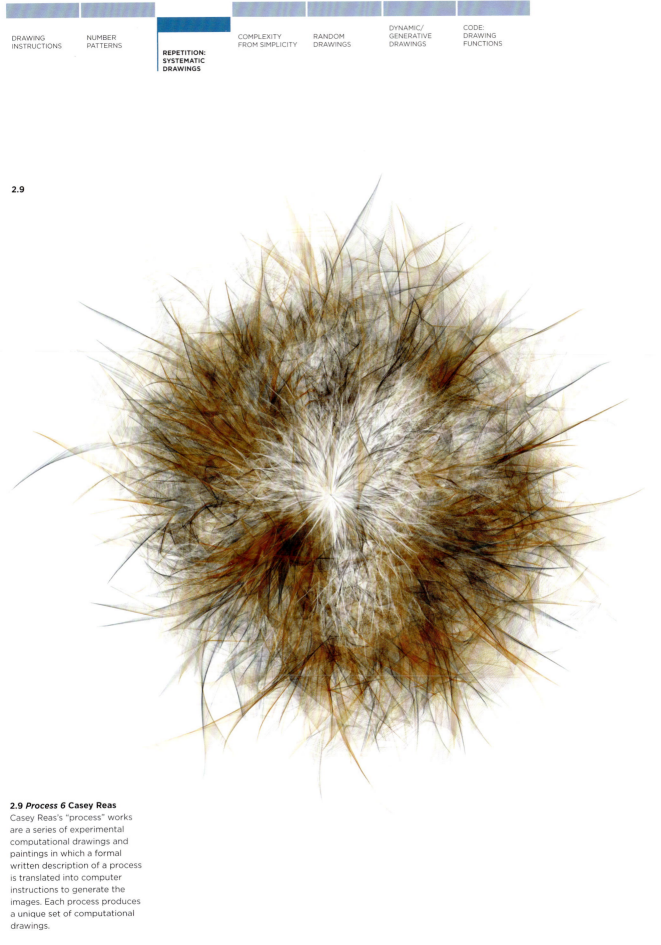

2.9 *Process 6* **Casey Reas**
Casey Reas's "process" works
are a series of experimental
computational drawings and
paintings in which a formal
written description of a process
is translated into computer
instructions to generate the
images. Each process produces
a unique set of computational
drawings.

EXEMPLAR

Moving Brands:
Logo for EMScom

Moving Brands are a design agency noted for innovation and experimentation within the arena of design for new, digital media. Their rebrand design of the EMScom logo highlights an innovative, experimental approach to graphic design that encompasses a range of disciplines within the graphic design area and showcases ways in which digital programming design can inform traditional graphic design.

The EMScom brand identity was developed from a visualization of the brand identity and subsequently used across print and screen media. A simple "reactive" grid of lines was programmed in Processing as an interactive, visual representation of the characteristics of the core identity of the company. Each individual line in the grid was programmed to be reactive to user mouse-clicks and responsive to the qualities of the lines around it, so that each line takes its orientation and weight from those surrounding it.

2.10

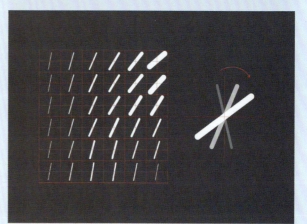

DRAWING
INSTRUCTIONS

NUMBER
PATTERNS

REPETITION:
SYSTEMATIC
DRAWINGS

COMPLEXITY
FROM SIMPLICITY

RANDOM
DRAWINGS

DYNAMIC/
GENERATIVE
DRAWINGS

CODE:
DRAWING
FUNCTIONS

2.11

COMMUNICATION
MANAGEMENT
EXECUTIVE EDUCATION

Generative/Dynamic Logos

Corporate identities are created as a detailed set of visual grids, rules, and structures that outline the circumstances and rules of their usage. By applying programming rules and instructions to set and manipulate their visual attributes, brand identities can be created as "dynamic," reactive logos—not only animated but also responsive to different types of data input. These "dynamic" logos become flexible, generative, living objects that express the values and characteristics of a brand in a range of playful, malleable, and highly customizable ways.

Many examples have been created that explore and experiment with the idea of translating (creating) dynamic number parameters to generate variations and visual systems for logo design.

2.10–11 EMScom Moving Brands
An interactive organic grid of lines, used as the basis for the visual identity of the EMScom brand, was created using Processing code. The visual structure worked as a strong, flexible base from which a range printed outcomes were produced.

COMPLEXITY
FROM SIMPLICITY

The sheer computational (number-crunching) ability of the computer means that the number of iterations or loops that can be performed completely overwhelms what would be possible any other way. Hundreds or even thousands of instructions and processes can be continually (and effortlessly) looped or iterated several times per second while the program runs. Thus, using this environment to draw can begin a process that can repeat and run—theoretically, at least—forever.

The ability of a computer program to infinitely repeat calculations and processes gives it an enormous potential for creating complex drawings and graphics. Just as a single paint stroke or pencil line, when repeatedly applied, can create an intricate drawing or diagram, simple geometric shapes, when computationally repeated and combined, can generate intricate digital forms. When computational shapes are plugged into a program that harnesses the vast processing ability of the computer to draw and change numbers and graphics, an infinite variety and combination of shapes is made possible. Combinations of circles, lines, and polygons can quickly be re-generated to create a huge variety of graphical forms. Programming instructions can be used to define initial rules and parameters, and a repetitive process allows drawings and designs to gradually grow and evolve. Minor changes to the drawing functions, when repeated, will generate changes to the drawing of lines, shapes, and graphics.

Programming loops, therefore, give designers the ability to generate complex drawings from a few simple instructions. A long list of drawing commands is unnecessary; a few drawing instructions can be recurrently executed hundreds or thousands of times. An initial design rule provides the starting conditions and parameters for the process. The visual complexity that can emerge from just a few initial instructions gives both the code and the drawing a kind of computational elegance, generating visual complexity from programmed simplicity. The combination of complexity and simplicity is an important and powerful idea that is often used by artists and designers when exploring the capacities of programming code.

EXEMPLAR

Universal Everything: Lovebytes Logo

Universal Everything used programming code to produce publicity material for Lovebytes, a digital arts organization based in Sheffield, UK. The design solution was based around a specially written generative drawing program that produced 20,000 unique variations of a single basic amoeba character that was then used as the image for 20,000 unique postcards and invites. The code repeated commands to adjust the specific attributes of each individual amoeba (its shape, texture, color, eye position, etc.). Although all were created from one generic computational template, each drawing was unique. Projects like this highlight the potential of computer code working with print processes in order to yield graphics of infinite variety.

DRAWING
INSTRUCTIONS

NUMBER
PATTERNS

REPETITION:
SYSTEMATIC
DRAWINGS

COMPLEXITY
FROM SIMPLICITY

RANDOM
DRAWINGS

DYNAMIC/
GENERATIVE
DRAWINGS

CODE:
DRAWING
FUNCTIONS

2.12

2.12 *Lovebytes*
Universal Everything
Repeatedly (and potentially
almost infinitely) applying
random computational
processes to a print-based
project produces a unique set of
generative postcards.

EXEMPLAR

Moving Brands: IO

In 2013, Moving Brands developed the visual identity and branding for Swisscom's stand-alone communication app. Although the final outcomes included many traditional types of print and screen media, an experimental engagement with generative code was used as a central part of the final design process and solution. The project is an interesting example of the way in which code can be used to create simple yet flexible visual programming "sketches" that can generate a dynamic set of brand assets.

Using Processing as a coding environment, the design team wrote a simple application that repeats a basic arc shape in a range of different spiral formations. The number values used to set the visual details (location, angle, color, etc.) of each repetitive pattern could be changed via a set of on-screen sliders that shifted the appearance of overall shape and form.

Even minor adjustments to the values resulted in large visual changes, and encouraged the designer to "play" with the programming system to generate a variety of outcomes. The visually generative program was therefore able to output an almost endless array of vibrant shapes and forms. Selected visuals produced by the program were saved and employed as both static and moving textures across the brand, including the app interface, website elements, printed artwork, and promotional video.

2.13

DRAWING
INSTRUCTIONS

NUMBER
PATTERNS

REPETITION:
SYSTEMATIC
DRAWINGS

**COMPLEXITY
FROM SIMPLICITY**

RANDOM
DRAWINGS

DYNAMIC/
GENERATIVE
DRAWINGS

CODE:
DRAWING
FUNCTIONS

2.13 iO Moving Brands

A specially built Processing tool allowed the designers of the visual identity for iO the chance to develop a range of generatively created static and moving textures that helped inform all aspects of the final design solution.

RANDOM DRAWINGS

If simple mathematical sequences generate visual predictability, then random numbers generate uncertainty and visual noise. The concept of "randomness" as a part of visual expression is important; it has been explored and experimented with in different ways by artists and designers. The most notable example probably comes from the American abstract expressionist movement of artists typified by Jackson Pollock, whose "drip" paintings have become a well-known symbol of artistic chance.

Introducing uncontrolled visual elements of chance or accident allows the artist to step outside the usual boundaries of conscious effort, move beyond visual predictability, and step into an area governed by other external, uncontrolled, or subconscious forces. The results are one-off pieces of work that contain elements of the unexpected. Elements of unpredictability bring their own kind of visual beauty, often associated with hand-made or non-mechanistic processes, and have even been introduced into the environment of graphics software. Special brush tools in Illustrator and Photoshop use elements of randomness to simulate the effect real-life painting tools.

The introduction of chance and accident ("randomness") does not mean, however, that the work is completely without the influence of the artist. Even in a random process, some of the visual parameters and attributes have to be set and defined by the artist or designer. For example, in Pollock's "drip" paintings, the artist selects the colored paints and his physical movements contribute to the creation of the lines. A "random" process therefore involves a balance between the controlled and the uncontrolled in

2.14

2.14 An example of one of Jackson Pollock's famous "drip" style paintings.

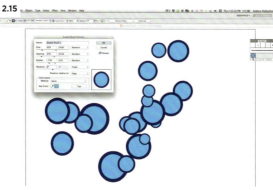

2.15

2.15 Illustrator screen shot
Elements of visual "randomness" are often desirable parts of a drawing or design. Illustrator, like many pieces of drawing software, includes the ability to randomize shapes and marks on the screen by adjusting the settings of the "scatter" brush.

which the artist sets the constraints and makes the final judgments (i.e., how much "randomness" to apply and when the piece is finished). Total randomness results in visual noise; however, when carefully applied and used within defined visual parameters (e.g., a limited color palette), the unexpected nature of the results can be interesting.

In the code environment, visual randomness is achieved numerically: Special programming functions generate random number values that can then be applied to one or many visual elements of the drawing. The shape, size, color, line weight, and line direction of a drawing can be generated randomly, producing different results and visual outcomes each time the program is run. The direct connections

among code, numbers, and visuals allow a direct link to be made between a randomly selected number value and a randomly changing visual element. Adding randomness into a code drawing is a simple but powerful way to generate an unpredictable set of visual designs subject to chance and random selection.

See Code section: Chaos: Random Patterns (page 60).

2.16

The designer defines "how much" randomness to use (the level of "chance" within the work) by specifying the range from which the numbers are selected and specifying which attributes are generated in this way. This is important because the results of pure (computational) randomness, in which all colors, shapes, and marks are randomly generated, produces uniformly messy results: the visual equivalent of "white noise." When applied carefully, elements of randomness and unpredictability can offer nuances of change and variance that generate subtle variations of visual change. Although the idea of randomness may seem to oppose artists' and designers' desire to maintain visual control, they value it; it provides nuance to graphics generated in the otherwise predictable and potentially formulaic computational environment.

When using code to create graphics, the designer has to embrace the idea of visual uncertainty. Relinquishing some control over details of the final visuals is an important part of the creative process.

2.16 *Process 16* Casey Reas
Although defined by a set of written and computational instructions, the outcomes from Casey Reas's computational "process" paintings have a tendency towards randomness that is an echo of Jackson Pollock's "drip" paintings.

EXEMPLAR

Holger Lippmann: Perlin Scape 1

Holger Lippmann is a German-based artist who uses programming (particularly Processing) as a significant part of his creative practice. The Perlin Scape series is based on a "perlin noise" algorithm: a function that generates a random series of number values that have a more naturalistic sequence than "purely" random numbers.

A randomly generated perlin number sequence is used to define the visual attributes (i.e., colors and angles) of a series of rectangles. The outcome of the process is a harmonic composition: a digital painting of a flowing wave of colored shapes. The use of computationally generated random number values gives the composition its naturalistic feel and means that each new version of the artwork is unique.

Perlin Noise

"Perlin noise" is an algorithm invented by Ken Perlin in the 1980s that produces a "naturalistic" sequence of random numbers. It is often applied to create organic-seeming textures, terrains, and shapes in the computer environment.

2.17

2.17 *Perlin Scape*
Holger Lippmann
The controlled randomness of the "Perlin noise" values gives a harmonic, naturalistic visual flow to the images.

DRAWING INSTRUCTIONS

NUMBER PATTERNS

REPETITION: SYSTEMATIC DRAWINGS

COMPLEXITY FROM SIMPLICITY

RANDOM DRAWINGS

DYNAMIC/ GENERATIVE DRAWINGS

CODE: DRAWING FUNCTIONS

EXEMPLAR

FIELD: 10,000 Digital Paintings

The innovative design studio Field created a series of 10,000 unique digital illustrations to use on printed promotional pieces to publicize the work of the independent paper manufacturer G. F. Smith. The studio used a randomized generative process to create an organic digital sculpture; each individual fragment from it became one of 10,000 images. The result is a set of vibrant, colorful paintings whose use of dynamically generated images pushes the boundaries and possibilities of digital print.

2.18 *10,000 Digital Paintings*
FIELD
A series of 10,000 unique illustrations generated by code processes and developed for use as cover artwork for G. F. Smith's paper brochure. The final design solution showcases the immense possibilities of digital print and generative design.

DYNAMIC/GENERATIVE DRAWINGS

Unlike a sketch fixed onto paper, or the digital animation fixed in time, a code-based graphic is dynamic (i.e., changeable and variable). The outcome of a code-generated drawing can be subject to change from external data information and can produce a range of surprising and unexpected results. The same piece of code run one hundred times can return one hundred slightly different results because numbers that define graphical attributes are dynamic and changeable, altering each time the code is run. Acting as a kind of data-driven visualization, computational drawings and designs can be generated from an array of numeric data sources, which opens up new creative possibilities for drawing and visualizing graphical information. Code-created drawings can be created from number values that are generated randomly or mathematically (as discussed), from mouse movement, user gesture and interaction, time data, audio feeds, or from many other externally sourced data sets.

In programming terminology, changeable data values are referred to as "variables." Variables are named containers for changing values and are commonly used to replace fixed numbers used to define a visual attribute of a drawing. Variables are at the heart of many programming concepts and provide the cornerstone for creating digitally dynamic and responsive images. Each time the program is run, new sets of visual outcomes are produced. The results can include a wide range of visual experiments; pleasant accidents and unexpected visual combinations emerge, with a range of graphical uses and applications.

See Code sections: Adding Variables (page 58) and Mouse Position: mouseX, mouseY (page 59).

A designer will create the overarching structure and parameters of the code but sets aside total control of the visual result by allowing the influence of variable, external data (e.g., random numbers, user generated data, or external data) to create specific elements of the visual output. Some initial ideas that imagine how variables and visuals can be linked together help to create a concept to define the parameters of the drawing. The initial concept can be very simple ("draw circles at the position of the mouse") or more complex; it may, for example, link color values to numbers that are fed in from an external data source.

Once a link between dynamic number values and visual parameters of the drawing have been created, the creative process becomes one of "fine-tuning" this relationship between the numbers and the visuals in order to generate the most pleasing set of outcomes. An experimental cycle of trial and error—a creative dialogue between the designer and the program—develops in which a balance and harmony between the "hard" numbers and code and the "soft" graphics is developed. The creative process is a "partnership" between the designer, who defines the concept and the structure, and the code, which allocates and uses specific data values.

Connecting variable values to visual attributes allows an image to become "dynamically" changeable. A huge variety of different numeric data sources can be used to generate graphics that can be used in a wide range of visual contexts and outcomes. Even simple connections between visuals and dynamically changeable number values can form rewarding and interesting visual results. The position of the mouse on screen, for example, is captured by two simple co-ordinate number values (mouseX, mouseY), which change as the user moves the mouse. Mouse movement can be linked to several visual attributes and used to change the position, size, or color of a shape. Connecting "dynamic" values to the visual properties of a graphic creates a simple, but direct, link between the user and an on-screen graphic, and can produce many interesting visual results.

DRAWING
INSTRUCTIONS

NUMBER
PATTERNS

REPETITION:
SYSTEMATIC
DRAWINGS

COMPLEXITY
FROM SIMPLICITY

RANDOM
DRAWINGS

DYNAMIC/
GENERATIVE
DRAWINGS

CODE:
DRAWING
FUNCTIONS

EXEMPLAR

Sagmeister and Walsh: Casa da Musica Identity

Created by Sagmeister and Walsh, the visual identity for Casa Da Musica, a center of music in Porto, Portugal, is a good example of how bespoke software can be used to inform a visually flexible and dynamic graphic identity.

The uniquely distinctive shape of the Rem Koolhass–designed building was used as a visual source from which a 3D logo was generated, viewable from a variety of different viewpoints and perspectives. New versions of the logo shape were created from individual views of the building. A bespoke software program was written as a "logo generator" to create unique versions of the logo informed by color values from a selected image (e.g., a photograph of a musician or staff from the venue). Color values are picked from seventeen specific points on the image and used to define the seventeen colored faces of the 3D logo shape. Each image therefore generates a unique set of colored visual identities based around the core logo shape that matches the colors of the original image. In this way, a dynamically flexible set of visual identities is created that has a clear visual link back to an original image. Each new set of logos can be used on a range of graphical outcomes associated with the venue to create unique promotional event posters or personalized business cards.

2.19

2.19 *Casa da Musica Identity*
Sagmeister & Walsh
Logo generator software was created to extract color from an image and then apply it to different versions of the logo. Individual versions of the logo are created that have a visual connection with the image.

Print Screen

When using code to create graphics, the images are generated at a low "screen" resolution that looks good on a monitor but is not good for printing at a large scale (e.g., to use as a graphic on a poster). Some programming languages include the ability to export the screen-generated graphics as large-scale images or even as pdf files, which can be opened and re-sized at any printer-friendly resolution. The Processing language, for example, includes a special library that makes it possible to write code-generated graphics as pdf files, and this is a useful way to generate graphics that can be scaled, sized, and output at very high resolutions. Details of the library are available as part of the Processing reference guide online here: https://processing.org/reference/libraries/pdf/

EXEMPLAR

IO: Here to There

The project Here to There explores a process that combines programming algorithms, processes, and concepts alongside hand-illustrated graphics to create a series of imaginative, digitally generated illustrations for children.

Inspired by the childhood memories of artworks on their bedroom walls, the designers Emily Gobeille and Theo Watson built their own suite of software tools (using openFrameworks), each of which explored computational concepts such as algorithm and cause and effect. The graphics each program produced became the basic building blocks of the posters; these were combined with hand-illustrated graphics of creatures and characters to create a hybrid story of two worlds: "City" and "Jungle." A wide variety of data sources were mined as numeric information to generate the drawings—for example, elevation data from a Hawaiian volcano and from the surface of the moon, as well as data taken from voice waveforms of the artists. The resultant illustrations are playful depictions of a bizarre fantasy of worlds; they mix computationally developed imagery with character design, narrative, and illustration to create the story of two visually striking environments. The final artworks were released as a limited run of prints.

Computational drawings can therefore generate compelling visual representations of data (movement, time, user interaction, etc.), making interesting new visual associations directed by programming rules and parameters. The links between dynamic data and graphical outcome are explored in more detail throughout the rest of this book.

2.20

2.20 *Here to There* **Design IO**
Illustrations for children's posters created from a mix of code-generated graphics and hand-drawn illustrations.

CODE: DRAWING FUNCTIONS

Many programming languages have their own vocabulary of pre-built drawing functions that allow the programmer to define and create simple shapes, points, and lines. Although basic, these simple elements form the basis of many computational drawings, and when repeated, layered, and combined can create intricate visual forms. The following is an outline of the basic drawing procedures used in Processing.

Creating the Canvas

It is useful to think of the on-screen "canvas" as a digital type of graph paper on which each pixel is a single square of the graph. The size of the drawing area (the canvas) is defined by a "size()" function, which sets the pixel width and height of the on-screen drawing area.

```
size (width, height);
// creates a drawing area of 640px by 480px
size (640, 480);
```

Drawing Shapes

Go to www.bloomsbury.com/richardson-data-driven, Chapter 2, and click on the project "Drawing Functions."

Processing includes a range of drawing functions that can be used to draw points, lines, circles, and squares. Each of these is created by simple programming functions that plot a shape on the x and y co-ordinate grid of the canvas.

The simplest shape is a single pixel dot, which can be drawn to the screen using the point() function. The function uses two number values, which set the x and y co-ordinate location of the dot.

```
point (x, y); // the point function
// draws a dot at the co-ordinate point x:100px,
y:150px`
point (100, 150);
```

A straight line is created by connecting two points together. The line() function takes the x, y co-ordinates of two points and joins them into a straight line;

```
// sample syntax
line (x1, y1, x2, y2);
// draws a line from x:100, y:150 to x:300, y:250
line (100, 150, 300, 250);
```

Other simple 2D shapes can be created by plotting and connecting more points. A triangle, for example, is created by the triangle() function, which connects three sets of x, y co-ordinate points.

```
// 3 sets of co-ordinate points create a triangle
triangle (x1, y1, x2, y2, x3, y3);
// connect the points (100, 50), (25, 120), (150,
140) into a triangle
triangle (100, 50, 25, 120, 150, 140);
```

Ellipses and rectangles are drawn by setting a single co-ordinate as the starting location for the shape (e.g., the center point of the ellipse or corner point of the rectangle) and using two other values to define the width and height of the shape.

DRAWING
INSTRUCTIONS

NUMBER
PATTERNS

REPETITION:
SYSTEMATIC
DRAWINGS

COMPLEXITY
FROM SIMPLICITY

RANDOM
DRAWINGS

DYNAMIC/
GENERATIVE
DRAWINGS

CODE:
DRAWING
FUNCTIONS

The ellipse() function draws ellipses and circles:

```
// set the x, y, width and height values
ellipse (x, y, w, h);
// draw an ellipse at x:70, y:60, width:40, height:30
ellipse (70, 60, 40, 30);
```

The rect() function draws rectangles and squares:

```
// set the x, y, width and height values of the
rectangle
rect (x, y, w, h);
rect (150, 200, 50, 70);
rect (150, 200, 100, 100); // a 100 pixel square
```

Circles and squares are drawn by using equal width and height numbers with the ellipse() and rect() functions.

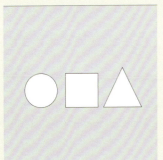

An example of the basic types of shapes that designers can create with shape drawing functions. These types of shapes are basic visual units of computational drawings.

TRY IT

Create a new Processing sketch.
Use the size() function to set the drawing area.
Explore each of the drawing functions (point, ellipse, line, and rect); use them to draw some simple computational drawings to the screen.

Color: fills and strokes

Go to www.bloomsbury.com/richardson-data-driven, Chapter 2, and click on the project "Adding Color."

Color, like many things in the computational environment, is precisely defined as number values. The simplest set of color values is the 256 shades of gray.

Grayscale values, moving from black to white, are defined by a single range of number values from 0 to 255, where 0 is "black," 255 is "white." All values in between are shades of gray, moving from dark grays (lowest numbers) to light grays (highest values).

Grayscale numbers can be used to change the color of elements on screen to specific shades of black and white.

Color used as the fill and outline of shapes is set with the fill() and stroke() functions. The background color of the canvas is set using the background() function.

```
// sets the background of the page to white
background (255);
// sets the outline (stroke) color to black
stroke (0);
fill (125); // sets the fill color to mid-gray
```

A much greater range of colors and shades are available by using the RGB color range, created by using three number values, each between 0 and 255, to represent amounts of red, green, and blue. Like the grayscale values, RGB values can be applied to change the color of the page, fills, or outlines.

```
// syntax examples:
background (r, g, b);
fill (r, g, b);
stroke (r, g, b);
```

By using numbers to digitally "mix" amounts of red, green, and blue, a designer can create any shade of color within the RGB spectrum. Bright red, for example, is defined by the RGB values of (255, 0, 0), which mix the "most" amount of red (255) with no green or blue (0, 0).

Other colors within the RGB spectrum can be mixed using combinations of these RGB values. Processing includes a color picker to help set the RGB numbers for any color. Once a fill or stroke value is set, it is applied to all subsequent shapes and lines, unless it is changed further down.

```
fill (13, 184, 216); // select blue as fill
ellipse (100, 200, 40, 40); // draw blue circle
fill (214, 104, 13); // change fill to orange
rect (300, 200, 50, 50); // draw orange square
```

The Color Selector in Processing allows the RGB (red, green, blue) values of any color to be found. There are similar tools available in most pieces of image-editing software.

Alpha values are percentage values (0 to 100) that can be added at the end of the RGB values as a fourth number to change the color transparency level.

```
// Syntax example:
fill (red, green, blue, ALPHA);
```

```
// bright red with a 50% alpha value
fill (255, 0, 0, 50);
```

TRY IT

Use fill() and stroke() to change the colors of shapes in your drawings.

Other visual attributes of a shape can be adjusted, including the width of the line or outline:

```
strokeWeight(5); // sets the weight of the outline
noStroke(); // removes all outlines
noFill(); // removes fill color
```

Adding variables

Go to www.bloomsbury.com/richardson-data-driven, Chapter 2, and click on the project "Variables."

Each of the drawing examples so far has used fixed number values in the ellipse() or rect() drawing function to set the location and size of each shape. Instead, however, of a fixed number value, using a variable number within the drawing function gives the shape more potential to be flexible and changeable. Once a variable is used within a function to draw a shape, altering the variable will automatically alter the shape. Once a number variable is created, it can be used in place of a fixed number in a shape function.

```
float xpos = 20;
float ypos = 10;
ellipse (xpos, ypos, 10, 10);
```

Altering or re-calculating the value of a variable will therefore change the drawing function in which it is used.

TRY IT

Create a number variable and use it in place of a fixed number in a shape drawing function.
Change the value of the variable to see how it affects the shape.
Create more variables to alter other elements of the shape.

Writing the code to change a variable and draw a shape inside a looping draw() element of a program will re-draw the resulting shape, and that repeated re-drawing can create a simple animated movement. For example, continually changing a variable that is used to set the x position of a shape will allow the shape to move horizontally across the screen.

```
float xpos = 10;
void draw() {
    ellipse (xpos, 50, 5, 5);
    xpos += 2;
}
```

DRAWING
INSTRUCTIONS

NUMBER
PATTERNS

REPETITION:
SYSTEMATIC
DRAWINGS

COMPLEXITY
FROM SIMPLICITY

RANDOM
DRAWINGS

DYNAMIC/
GENERATIVE
DRAWINGS

CODE:
DRAWING
FUNCTIONS

TRY IT

Re-create the Processing example above.
Add a new variable and use it to set the y location of the ellipse.
Add a line of code to change the value of the new variable.
Create additional variables to alter the width and height of the shape.

```
Mouse Position: mouseX, mouseY
```

Variable number values can be changed by data from other sources, such as user input. System variables mouseX and mouseY are really simple and useful variables that grab the screen location of the mouse as it moves across the screen. They can be used to create objects that respond to users' mouse movements. The following example will repeatedly draw a circle at the location of the mouse.

```
void draw() {
   ellipse (mouseX, mouseY, 50, 50);
}
```

Repetition and Drawing with "For" Loops

Go to www.bloomsbury.com/richardson-data-driven, Chapter 2, and click on the project "For Loops."

"For" loops repeat lines of code and create predictable number sequences that can be used to repeat graphics in a structured and orderly way and create repetitive shapes and patterns. A single drawing function inside a "for" loop will be repeated several times and create several drawings.

In this example, the "counter" variable (i) is used to draw 40 lines, using the value of "i" to alter the x position of each line in a sequential manner. As the value of "i" counts up from 0 to 40, so the x position of each line also increments from 0 to 40.

```
// as i changes, so does the x position of the both
ends of the line
for (int i=0; i<40; i++) {
   line (i, 10, i, 100);
}
```

Slight adjustments to the line function code alter the distance between the lines.

```
// draw each line 10 pixels apart
for (int i=0; i<40; i++) {
   line (i*10, 10, i*10, 100);
}
```

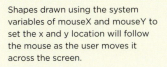

Shapes drawn using the system variables of mouseX and mouseY to set the x and y location will follow the mouse as the user moves it across the screen.

Drawing shapes with a "for" loop creates a regular sequence of shapes. In this instance, lines are created in a regular sequence. Altering one of the number values— for example, the x location of the top of the line—creates a simple rhythmical pattern.

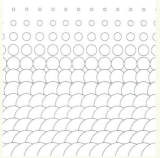

Nesting two "for" loops, one inside another, is used to create a "grid" of shapes. Simple adjustments to the size of the shape alter the overall shape patter

TRY IT

Create your own "for" loop.
Include a println() command to output a number sequence.
Add a drawing function and use the loop to generate a regimented sequence of shapes.

"For" loops are useful for generating graphics:

• "For" loops can be used to create ordered sequential graphics.
• A "for" loop can generate 100s or 1000s of items in a few lines of code.
• Nesting loops, one inside another, can be used to generate a structured row and column "grid" of shapes.

Chaos: Random Patterns

Go to www.bloomsbury.com/richardson-data-driven, Chapter 2, and click on the project "Random."

In contrast to the ordered number sequences created by a "for" loop, other programming functions can be used to generate less predictable number sequences that can be applied to create visual variety.

In Processing, the random() function is used to generate a random number from within a given range. The number range is expressed within the brackets either as a single (maximum) value or as two numbers (minimum and a maximum) values. If one number is used, 0 is used as the default minimum number.

```
// generates a number between 0 and "max"
random (max);
// generates a number between 0 and 20
random (20);
random (min, max);
// generates a number between 10 and 20
random (10, 20);
// generates a number between -40 and 40
random (-40, 40);
```

Each time the random() function is called, it generates a new value. Applying a random number to a variable allows the value of the variable to generate unpredictable number values. Random values can be used to generate/alter any numeric property (e.g., size, position, color, etc.). The following example draws a circle at a random x, y location each time it is run.

```
float x = random(400); // create a random x value
float y = random(200); // create a random y value
// draw a circle at the x, y location
ellipse (x, y, 20, 20);
```

DRAWING
INSTRUCTIONS

NUMBER
PATTERNS

REPETITION:
SYSTEMATIC
DRAWINGS

COMPLEXITY
FROM SIMPLICITY

RANDOM
DRAWINGS

DYNAMIC/
GENERATIVE
DRAWINGS

**CODE:
DRAWING
FUNCTIONS**

TRY IT

Use the random() function to create a random number. Apply it to one element of a drawing function (e.g., width).
Add more random elements and apply to a color value.
Put the code within a draw() loop to keep re-drawing the random shapes.

A random function combined with a "for" loop can be used to generate a lot of random shapes. The following example generates 100 circles drawn at random locations at random sizes. Each iteration of the "for" loop generates new values and draws a new shape with a new size and location.

```
// use a "for" loop to repeat the random drawing of
a circle
for (int i=0; i<100; i++) {
    float x = random (300);
    float y = random (400);
    float w = random (5, 50);
    ellipse (x, y, w, w);
}
```

Remember:

• Randomness is visually useful, but needs to be controlled.
• Random numbers can be applied to any numeric element.
• A new random value is created each time the random() function is called.

 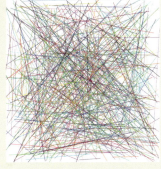

The random() function creates unpredictable numbers, which can be applied to any visible attribute of a shape, including color (using random numbers for the red, green, and blue values).

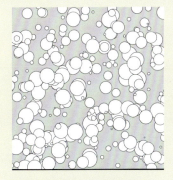 

Random lines and shapes can be quickly created by repeating the random() function to draw shapes in new locations and in different sizes.

TRY IT

Use a "for" loop to generate 100 shapes.
Use the random() function to randomize the features of each shape, including size, location, and color.

Translate and Rotate

Go to www.bloomsbury.com/richardson-data-driven, Chapter 2, and click on the project "Translate and Rotate."

Plotting shapes on the grid of the screen can be done in the usual way. For example:

```
// draw a shape at x:10 and y:20
ellipse (10, 20, 5, 5);
```

A translation is a way of moving the co-ordinate grid of the stage, meaning that shapes drawn after translation has happened are shifted to a new place on the screen.

However, drawings in processing can also be "translated." This means that rather than moving the shape to a given screen co-ordinate, a translation moves the co-ordinate grid of the screen. A translate() function has the effect of shifting the (0,0) origin point to a new place. This effect of "moving the graph paper" means that the positions of all the shapes on the grid are shifted. The translate() function uses two values to shift the co-ordinate grid of the screen.

```
translate(x, y); // syntax example
```

The following example draws a shape before the screen grid has been translated and after, illustrating how the function works:

```
// draw a shape
ellipse (10, 20, 5, 5);
// translate the grid of the screen
translate (50, 50);
// draw a shape on the translated screen
ellipse (10, 20, 5, 5);
```

Even though the code for drawing the two shapes is the same, the second shape is drawn after the drawing grid has been moved 50 pixels across and down. This has the visual effect of drawing the second shape further along and down the screen, at the co-ordinates of 60, 70.

Translate functions are often used with pushMatrix() and popMatrix() functions. These are used to save and re-set the shifted co-ordinate grid, so that the drawing area is reset back after the translation has happened.

In the following example, the ellipse is drawn on the "translated" grid. The pushMatrix() and popMatrix() functions are used to save and reset the grid, so that the rectangles are drawn on the normal co-ordinate grid.

```
rect (10, 20, 5, 5);
// save the current grid position
pushMatrix();
translate (50, 50);
// draw a shape with translation
ellipse (10, 20, 5, 5);
// return back to the normal grid
popMatrix();
// draw a shape on the "normal" grid
rect (30, 30, 5, 5);
```

TRY IT

Draw shapes before and after a translate() function to see how this works.
Add a pushMatrix() and popMatrix() to reset the grid and draw more shapes.

Using translate() is most useful when rotating shapes in Processing. Rotating a shape is done by using the rotate command and then drawing a shape:

```
rotate (radians (45)); // rotate grid by 45 degrees
rect (0, 0, 20, 20); // draw a shape
```

DRAWING
INSTRUCTIONS

NUMBER
PATTERNS

REPETITION:
SYSTEMATIC
DRAWINGS

COMPLEXITY
FROM SIMPLICITY

RANDOM
DRAWINGS

DYNAMIC/
GENERATIVE
DRAWINGS

CODE:
DRAWING
FUNCTIONS

Processing uses radians rather than degrees for rotation. The radians() function converts the angle into radians for us.

The rotate function rotates the grid on which the shape is drawn, so when a shape is rotated, it is done so around the origin point of the screen grid x:0, y:0. To place a shape in the middle of the screen and get it to rotate around its center point, the screen has to be translated first. The sequence of commands is: 1) translate the co-ordinate grid; 2) rotate the grid; 3) draw the shape.

The following is an example of how this works.

```
pushMatrix();
translate (50, 50); // move the grid
rotate (radians (45)); // rotate the grid
rect (0, 0, 10, 10); // draw the shape
popMatrix();
```

The translate function shifts the grid of the stage, which allows shapes to be rotated around a center point. A series of rotated shapes can create a simple spiral.

Notice how the shape function plots it at 0, 0. Because the screen has been translated, 0, 0 now appears to be in the middle of the screen at (50, 50). This is all done inside the pushMatrix() and popMatrix() functions so that any subsequent drawings will be placed on the grid as normal.

TRY IT

Apply the translate() and rotate() functions to rotate a simple shape.

CHAPTER THREE
GROWTH AND FORM

"The harmony of the world is made manifest in Form and Number."

D'Arcy Thompson

NATURE AS INSPIRATION

The environment of the natural, physical world and the environment of the digital, interactive world have much in common. Many of the basic concepts that govern the growth and development of organic life inspire the shapes and movements of "virtual" environments. Code gives "life" to digital objects, adding individual behaviors and characteristics to otherwise inanimate images. Designers and programmers use code to create their own digital "life forms": Lines and shapes emerge within the confines of a computationally generated world. Virtual simulations of real-life environmental forces—growth, movement, interaction, and decay—propel those forms. The link between virtual and digital worlds is such that designers commonly borrow the language of the natural world to describe the attributes and characteristics of their interactive creations. The screen is an "environment"; objects are often referred to as having "life" or "health" or the ability to "spawn" new shapes. Programmed interactive objects are given "behaviors"; they "grow," possess "structure," and enjoy the attributes of digital movement and life.

Computational designers therefore often look beyond the traditional landscape of graphic design and turn toward the natural world as a source of creative inspiration and reference. Naturally occurring behaviors, movement, and textures provide a wealth of visual information that sparks ideas. Their observation and documentation can form a key part of the visual and conceptual research and development process. The shapes and structures found in plants, trees, ferns, and fungus; the arcs and curves of leaves and shells; and the movements observed in a flock of birds or a school of fish can provide the creative springboard from which interactive digital concepts take flight.

Personal observations are not the only possible starting points; scientific diagrams, photographs, and illustrations also provide inspiration for interactive and generative ideas. The descriptions of historical and contemporary scientists seeking to order the forms of botanical and biological matter provide a rich source of visual information that continues to inspire and inform the work of many digital artists. The drawings of the German biologist Ernst Haeckel in his book *Art Forms of Nature* (1899) and the ideas, diagrams, and observations of the biologist D'Arcy Wentworth Thompson in his work *On Growth and Form* (1917), for example, have inspired work by contemporary code-based designers.

3.2

3.2 Sunflower and Flocking Birds
Shapes and forms found in nature—for example, in the spiral of a sunflower or the formation of flocking birds—contain their own kind of organic rhythm and beauty that have been a significant source of inspiration for generations of artists and designers.

NATURE AS INSPIRATION

DRAWING
AS GROWTH

ORGANIC
SHAPES:
SPIRALS
AND WAVES

COMPLEX
MATHEMATICAL
MODELS

DIGITAL
ECO-SYSTEMS

ENVIRONMENTAL
FORCES: GRAVITY,
ELASTICITY

SPOTLIGHT ON
DANIEL BROWN

CODE:
DIGITAL
ENVIRONMENTS

3.3

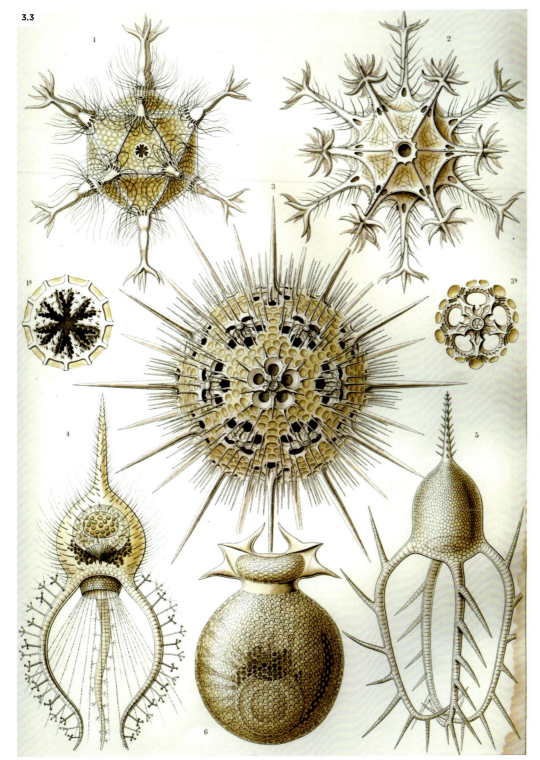

3.3 *Biological illustration*
Ernst Haeckel
Ernst Haeckel was a nineteenth-century German biologist, naturalist, and artist who studied the genealogical origin of many life forms. The detailed illustrations in his book *Art Forms of Nature* (1899) bridged the gap between science and art and proved to be a highly influential source in both architecture and design.

The natural world not only provides an important source of visual inspiration for interactive design; it also provides inspiration as an organized evolving system of growth that generates complex forms, patterns, and behaviors. Nature, like code, works according to an intricate and well-defined set of patterns and rules that govern the way in which plants, flowers, trees, birds, fish, insects, and others develop. Understanding the rules, structures, and growth patterns of organic life can inspire and inform digital and computational designers by showing how a repeatable "template" of simple rules and instructions can be applied to generate complicated forms.

Just as the seed of a plant contains a genetic code to determine the shape, pattern, and structure of each species (i.e., the number, size, and frequency of branches, leaves, and flowers), so also a set of programming instructions act as type of "digital seed" used to define computational rules from which digital shapes emerge and grow. A single seed-type generates a set of plants that, despite generic similarities, grow with its own subtle set of individual characteristics and variations; no two flowers or trees are exactly identical. Similarly, variations embedded within digital code means that each version of the code can produce uniquely varied results. The concept of a repeating, self-generating system of growth from which a rich variety of drawings can "grow" and emerge provides an important rich source of inspiration for artists and designers using code to draw.

3.4

NATURE AS
INSPIRATION

**DRAWING
AS GROWTH**

ORGANIC
SHAPES:
SPIRALS
AND WAVES

COMPLEX
MATHEMATICAL
MODELS

DIGITAL
ECO-SYSTEMS

ENVIRONMENTAL
FORCES: GRAVITY,
ELASTICITY

SPOTLIGHT ON
DANIEL BROWN

CODE:
DIGITAL
ENVIRONMENTS

DRAWING AS GROWTH

**3.4 *Dual Gardens* ART+COM
*Studios***
The growth of a large-scale
digital "garden" of plants
and flowers is governed by
computational instructions that
replicate the organic shapes and
patterns of flowers, fronds, and
leaves.

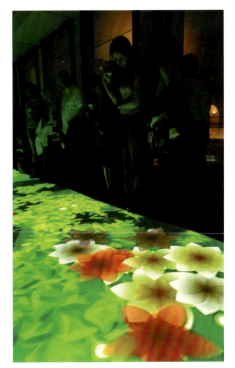

Code-generated drawings, like organic life, do not appear all at once, but develop gradually over time. The process is similar to planting a seed and watching it grow: lines, colors, and forms emerge gradually. They spread across the canvas of the screen like a digital organic form. The evolution of a code-driven drawing is a significant part of the experience and process of using code, which opens up interesting new ways of generating work.

Traditional software drawing tools allow designers to make closely considered design decisions, in which the details of a composition can be carefully controlled and edited. Unlike conventional digital works, drawings created by code are subject to much wider levels of uncertainty. Computational rules determine the overall conditions for the development of a drawing without precisely defining the exact outcome. Individual visual attributes (e.g., the specific direction, movement, shape, color, or size of a line) can be created as variable elements, the values of which are generated and changed while the program runs and the drawing grows. Code creates visuals that develop in unexpected ways, producing results that can be surprising both to the viewer and to the programmer.

Just as in the natural world no two shapes are identical, so it is that code allows designers to generate tens or hundreds of variations around the same shape. Rather than having a fixed design vision or outcome in mind, the designer / programmer may instead start with a concept that is the "seed": an instruction that forms the basis of the program. The concept could be based on observation of

a natural form, rhythm, or pattern (e.g., "branching line sprouts two more lines") or could be more abstract. By repeatedly looping a drawing instruction, an organic shape can grow. Small variable or "random" elements can be added into the calculations that subtly change the quality of each line or shape, giving each one its own naturalistic nuances. Altering, or adding variation to, the base concept will output a variety of interesting and surprising results around the core theme. The designer can modify the rules without fully knowing what effects the changes may have on the outcome when the code is run; the same drawing program can produce a wide range of new and unexpected visual outcomes each time.

EXEMPLAR

Conditional Design Group

The Conditional Design Group is an experimental, research-based, graphic design collective that explores ways of generating drawings and artifacts by using self-imposed conditions and rules of play to create organic visual outcomes. Using only non-digital materials (pens, paint, clay, tape, etc.), groups of participants engage in playful activities, taking turns to add to a drawing according to a pre-defined set of "rules." The rules of an activity provide defined limits to the design process but also allow participants to fully and wildly explore the visual possibilities within those boundaries of play. The result is a series of "generative" designs that emerge from shared processes of chance, time, and instruction.

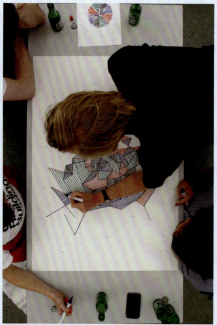

3.5 *Making of Hatching*
Conditional Design

NATURE AS
INSPIRATION

**DRAWING
AS GROWTH**

ORGANIC
SHAPES:
SPIRALS
AND WAVES

COMPLEX
MATHEMATICAL
MODELS

DIGITAL
ECO-SYSTEMS

ENVIRONMENTAL
FORCES: GRAVITY,
ELASTICITY

SPOTLIGHT ON
DANIEL BROWN

CODE:
DIGITAL
ENVIRONMENTS

This kind of "generative" development of a drawing, which is both regulated by rules and also "open" to play, randomness, exploration, and interpretation, mirrors the processes, concepts, and procedures used in programming code. Although the materials are physical rather than digital, and the lines are drawn by hand, rather than by a computer, the similarities are clear. Written rules act as the "program" and the participants act as the computer, translating and executing the instructions. Numbering the instructions, "taking turns," and giving precise parameters for the drawings (e.g., defining one color per person or stating that circles must be between 2cm and 5cm) makes sure that the creative actions occur within defined parameters and in an orderly sequence—as they do in a computer program. The individual creativity of the participant drawing "within the rules" of the activity simulates the elements of variability and chance embedded into code processes. The process sets rules that are carried out with time and chance as variables. The outcomes of the process are wonderfully varied and random; they translate the concepts of a computer program into the physical world of markers, pens, and paper.

3.6

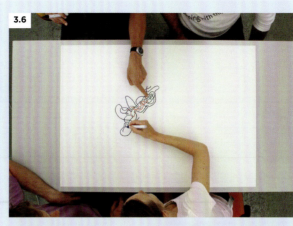

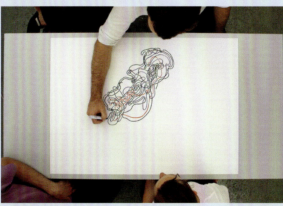

**3.6 *Making of Knots*
Conditional Design**
The rule-based systems of drawing devised by Conditional Design allow participants to engage in a process of image making in which the drawings emerge as a shared playful experience. Combining defined rules with individuals' choices, it mirrors the process of a computational system from which shapes emerge and grow.

ORGANIC SHAPES:
SPIRALS AND WAVES

Organic patterns are not chaotic or random; even the most complex-looking organic form contains an orderly sequence of repeating pattern and structure.

The movement of birds, the shape a leaf, or the spiral of a snail's shell can be mathematically described by sequences of numbers. The connection between nature and mathematics has informed and inspired generations of artists and designers and has, for a long time, been explored by mathematicians, scientists, and philosophers keen to numerically describe and unravel the numeric beauty and complexity behind the forms of nature. A particularly famous example of an organic number pattern is the Fibonacci sequence. Observed by a mathematician in the thirteenth century, the Fibonacci pattern of numbers is generated from a numeric calculation in which the last 2 numbers of the sequence are added to obtain the next number: 1, 1, 2, 3, 5, 8, 13, 21, 34, 55 . . . and so on. The relationship between each of these apparently random numbers is used to generate the Fibonacci Spiral (by the "golden ratio"), a pattern that is observable in many naturally occurring organic shapes, including sea shells, branching plants, seeds, leaves, and flower petal arrangements.

3.7 Shell spiral
The spiral shape found is a shell is a naturally occurring example of the Fibonacci number pattern.

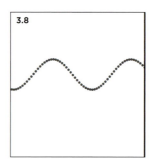

3.8 Sine wave
A sine wave is a computationally generated shape. The oscillating values that "bounce" between a minimum and maximum number generate a regular, flowing waveform. This type of wave can be applied to drawing lines or creating movement.

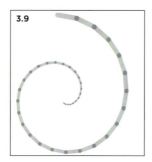

3.9 An example of a spiral shape generated by re-calculating the angle and length of a line.

Other number sequences generated by similar formal mathematical functions can be used to generate aesthetically pleasing shapes and lines that reflect the movement found in the natural environment. An example of this is the mathematical "sine" function. The sine calculation, originally used in Pythagoras calculations to work out the properties of a triangle, also generates a pattern of (oscillating) number values which, when plotted along a line, generate organic-looking wave shapes and forms.

See Code section: Sine Wave (page 88).

Computational programs often draw by repeating procedures to move an object (as a virtual "pen") across the screen; the "trail" of the path of movement leaves behind a line on the screen. Repeated mathematical calculations used to move and re-position the location of the "pen" create organic-looking arcs, curves, or swirls. A drawing function that, for example, repeatedly increases the angle for each location of the "pen" will draw a line that gradually spirals inwards. Similarly, numbers generated by a mathematical calculation like a Fibonacci sequence or a sine function can be used to create a flowing line drawing that mirrors the graceful elegance of a leaf or petal shape.

Number patterns applied to code-generated graphics create visually pleasing rhythms and patterns that mirror the shapes and movements of the natural environment.

NATURE AS
INSPIRATION

DRAWING
AS GROWTH

ORGANIC
SHAPES:
SPIRALS
AND WAVES

COMPLEX
MATHEMATICAL
MODELS

DIGITAL
ECO-SYSTEMS

ENVIRONMENTAL
FORCES: GRAVITY,
ELASTICITY

SPOTLIGHT ON
DANIEL BROWN

CODE:
DIGITAL
ENVIRONMENTS

COMPLEX MATHEMATICAL MODELS

More recently, computer-based mathematical systems have been developed that accurately and realistically simulate the repeating patterns of complex botanical growth (e.g., plants, weeds, yeast, fungi). These systems are applied to scientific study within systems biology and also extensively used within computer game technology to generate realistic environmental landscapes and terrain. Although technical and somewhat specialist in nature, computer modeling systems highlight important principles of organic growth that can be computationally replicated, providing ideas and inspiration for designers. The following is a brief overview of some of the concepts behind the main systems for computer-generated organic growth. Although they are do not need to be followed exactly, they reveal some important and interesting features.

Recursion

Programming structure and organic structure share the same tendency towards recursion. Recursion is a self-referencing, self-repeating process; part of the process includes an instruction back to the original, which creates a (potentially infinite) circular loop. There is a well-known joke about the dictionary definition that illustrates the concept in action:

Recursion (noun) See "Recursion."

Structures that display the visible properties of recursion are those that show characteristics of "self-similarity"; that is, each small part of the shape is exactly or approximately similar to its overall shape. Recursive structures, therefore, most commonly occur in the self-repeating shapes of organic forms, such as trees and rocks. Ferns are especially good examples of recursive shapes; each tiny frond and leaf of the fern is a similar, smaller version of the overall fern shape.

Recursive drawing functions written into code are therefore those that contain instructions to re-draw themselves, creating (infinitely) self-repeating patterns. There is a shared visual link between structured organic elements of the natural world and graphics created from recursive (looped) programming processes. They both display visual self-similarity.

3.10 Recursive shapes are often found in nature, especially in plants. In ferns, for instance, the whole shape is a large replica of each of the small individual sections.

3.11 *Bloom* **Robert Hodgin** Recursive processes can be used in code to create a branching structure of plant-like shapes. The branching structure of a tree is created by a "recursive" rule that repeats a simple instruction for each branch to create a number of smaller branches. Starting with a single line (branch), the rule is repeated, and the tree shape is created. This is a type of "fractal" geometry. Slight alterations to the way the branches occur change the appearance of the overall plant, allowing the system to generate many different shapes.

EXEMPLAR

Holger Lippmann: Cloud Forest

Cloud Forest is a series of generative trees created by the digital programmer and artist Holger Lippmann. Lippmann uses a recursive, generative code (Processing) to create a series of complex, highly intricate digital drawings. The level of detail, subtlety, and complexity in each of the drawings gives each piece the qualities of a painting rather than a computer-generated image. At the core of the work is a simple tree-branching (recursive) algorithm. The artist has carefully changed and adjusted the parameters and "settings" of the drawing algorithm, altering parameters that determine size, positioning, and transparency to achieve results that are closest to his vision for the final image. Working in this way is less like being a programmer and more like being an artist or a painter—experimenting with a process, fine-tuning the material (code), and continually making adjustments and aesthetic judgments to achieve the desired visual results. Lippmann himself describes the process of using this code as similar to dancing or improvising music, from which the final work evolves.

3.12 *Cloud Forest-Nebelwald*
Holger Lippmann
The generative tree compositions created by a recursive branching process possess a visual lightness suggestive of a traditional drawing or painting.

NATURE AS
INSPIRATION

DRAWING
AS GROWTH

ORGANIC
SHAPES:
SPIRALS
AND WAVES

**COMPLEX
MATHEMATICAL
MODELS**

DIGITAL
ECO-SYSTEMS

ENVIRONMENTAL
FORCES: GRAVITY,
ELASTICITY

SPOTLIGHT ON
DANIEL BROWN

CODE:
DIGITAL
ENVIRONMENTS

Koch Snowflake

Recursive functions allow designers to repeat and re-draw simple shapes in ways that increase complexity. The Koch snowflake is a complex shape developed by repeating a simple set of drawing instructions. It is an example of a fractal shape—that is, a mathematical shape that repeats at different scales. The Koch snowflake is constructed by starting with an equilateral triangle and recursively adding triangles to each of its sides. The repetition of this process creates an increasingly complex snowflake-like shape. Variations of the form can be created by applying the same process to a range of different types of shapes

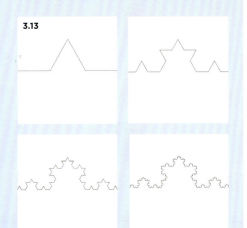

3.13

3.13 A Koch snowflake example
By repeating the line-drawing instruction, the fractal shape gradually gets more complex.

L Systems

An L system (Lindenmayer system) is a set of written rules that simulates growth by representing plant structure as an expanding series of letters. L systems describe biological growth as a formal grammatical structure.

A letter (usually A or B) represents a part of the plant (e.g., a left or right branch). Starting with a single letter, a few simple rules are used to re-generate the starting letter into an increasingly long sequence, adding new "branches" each turn. A computer program can then interpret each letter as a new line or branch, creating an overall branching plant structure that corresponds to the growing letter sequence. For example, if we begin with the letter "A" and the rule that for each turn, "A" becomes "AB" and "B" becomes "A," then the following sequence is created:

rule 1: A becomes AB
rule 2: B becomes A
turn 1: A
turn 2: AB
turn 3: ABA
turn 4: ABAAB

After each generation of the plant, the rules are applied again and the sequence added to. The result is an evolving letter sequence that can be visually interpreted as the growth of a natural form.

3.14

3.14 L-System example
When interpreted by a drawing machine, the string of characters generated by an L-System creates a series of plant-like shapes and forms.

DIGITAL ECO-SYSTEMS

Programming environments are self-contained digital eco-systems: abstract environments within which the programmer defines rules of movement, growth, and interaction. Just as a computer game environment has its own self-contained characteristics that determine how objects and characters move and interact, so each programming environment contains its own rules, defined by the programmer, that govern the way in which objects on the screen move, grow, and interact. These rules can be naturalistic, echoing behaviors of the physical world, or invented entirely from the imagination of the creator. The screen is a "blank canvas" in which the designer can "play god," defining the specific characteristics of the new environment.

Determining the "rules of play" for the environment is therefore an important part of the creative process, giving the work its focus and foundation. Digital environments may draw their rules from those that guide the evolution of a set of microorganisms, the movement of bubbles, or flocking behaviors of birds.

3.15

3.15 *Lightweeds*
Simon Heijdens
Projections of digital plants that grow and move within indoor spaces inreaction to environmental conditions outside.

NATURE AS INSPIRATION

DRAWING AS GROWTH

ORGANIC SHAPES: SPIRALS AND WAVES

COMPLEX MATHEMATICAL MODELS

DIGITAL ECO-SYSTEMS

ENVIRONMENTAL FORCES: GRAVITY, ELASTICITY

SPOTLIGHT ON DANIEL BROWN

CODE: DIGITAL ENVIRONMENTS

EXEMPLAR

Simon Heijdens: Lightweeds

Simon Heijden's project "Lightweeds" is an interesting example of how the digital environment can be an inspiration and a reflection of the natural world. Applying concepts inspired by the changing rhythms of growth, life, and decay present in organic matter, the work consists of a series of digital light projections that look like plants that grow taller and bend in the breeze. Often situated within an urban interior space, the presence of digital botanical forms that self-seed and undulate creates a sharp contrast to the controlled environments and architecture of modern spaces: a reminder of the lost presence of nature in daily life.

The digital plants grow from code that mirrors the growth patterns and structures of organic life. Code-generated "seeds" determine the genetic structure and behavior of each plant. All plants generated from the same family are generated by the same seed and therefore grow and act according to a shared "genetic" code. Each digital plant grows, lives, and dies in accordance with its digital seed. The plants even pollinate new plants, generating further growth. Information about the outside weather conditions (humidity, wind, and temperature) and the movement of people in front of the projection is translated into data that determines how the digital plants move and develop. The line between the digital and the organic blurs as the digital projections undulate and propagate in response to real environmental conditions.

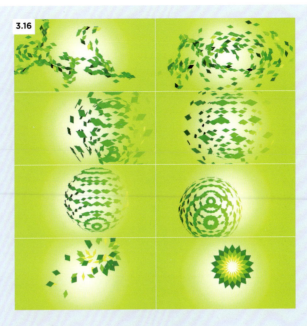

3.16

3.16 *Interactive Logograph* **Golan Levin**
An example of an early experiment in creating an interactive logograph. The BP logo is re-imagined as a dynamic field of individual shapes that collectively move in response to user interaction, gradually reforming to create the logo. The group behavior of the shapes mirror the organic, naturalistic movement of living creatures as they flock and swarm together.

Life-Like Behaviors

Code can be used to construct and apply naturalistic behaviors to individual graphical objects or groups of them, transforming digital shapes, letters, or lines into interactive and reactive objects. Behaviors give "life" to objects on screen, transforming them into digital organisms, allowing them to move, grow, change, interact with other objects, and even spawn and re-generate new shapes and forms. Graphics with these kinds of behavioral qualities become digital versions of simple life forms: plants, seeds, or living cell organisms.

Just as a family or species of living things share common attributes and behaviors, so groups of digital objects can inherit and share behavioral patterns. Object oriented programming (OOP) allows programmers to create groups of digital objects that share core functions and define a common set of generic behaviors (e.g., the ability to grow) while allowing each object the capacity to maintain its own individual attributes and aspects of its own "personality" (e.g., the specific rate of growth). Digital objects can therefore be created that, although they have their own individual attributes, can act and move with a common purpose, a kind of shared "group mentality," creating a pattern of motion that replicates natural phenomena such as the way birds flock and fish swim.

See Code section: Objects and Groups (page 93).

EXEMPLAR

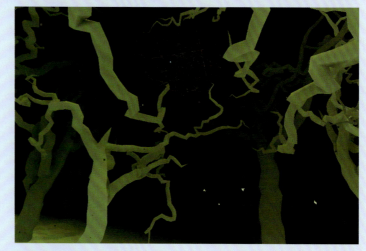

3.17 *PolyFauna* **Radiohead, Nigel Godrich, Stanley Donwood, and Universal Everything**
An experimental, immersive audio-visual environment for iOS and Android inhabited by computationally generated life forms.

NATURE AS
INSPIRATION

DRAWING
AS GROWTH

ORGANIC
SHAPES:
SPIRALS
AND WAVES

COMPLEX
MATHEMATICAL
MODELS

**DIGITAL
ECO-SYSTEMS**

ENVIRONMENTAL
FORCES: GRAVITY,
ELASTICITY

SPOTLIGHT ON
DANIEL BROWN

CODE:
DIGITAL
ENVIRONMENTS

Radiohead, Nigel Godrich, Stanley Donwood and Universal Everything Polyfauna

Described as a "a living, breathing, growing touchscreen environment" and inspired by atmospheric landscape paintings from J. W. Turner to Peter Doig, as well as the computational life forms of Carl Sims, PolyFauna is the result of a creative collaboration among Radiohead, Nigel Godrich, Stanley Donwood, and Universal Everything.

Built using the Unity engine and programmed in C#, the app presents an immersive audio-visual digital environment of primitive life, weather, sunsets, mountains, and forests. The ambient abstract environment is populated with computationally generated life forms. Variations of music, weather, color palette, moon phase, and creature species offer the user a unique set of encounters each time it is used. The digital environment is explored through gesture and movement, the internal camera within the space keeps moving forward, and movement left and right is achieved by physical rotations of the body. The project explores uses of computationally generated digital life and organic growth to create an immersive user experience.

EXEMPLAR

3.18

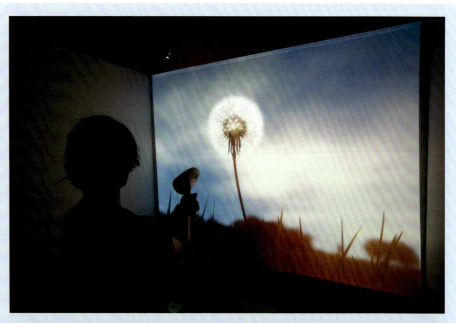

Sennep and Yoke: Dandelion Interactive

The movement of dandelion seeds as they get blown in the breeze is replicated digitally in this beautifully playful interactive installation. Users interact with a projection of a dandelion by using a hairdryer to blow seeds from it. The seeds drift away on a virtual breeze until none remain; then they reform and begin again. Code is used to mimic the movement of seeds floating on a breeze and create an experience resonant of childhood. Digital code translates interaction with the natural world into a poetic, immersive digital experience.

NATURE AS
INSPIRATION

DRAWING
AS GROWTH

ORGANIC
SHAPES:
SPIRALS
AND WAVES

COMPLEX
MATHEMATICAL
MODELS

**DIGITAL
ECO-SYSTEMS**

ENVIRONMENTAL
FORCES: GRAVITY,
ELASTICITY

SPOTLIGHT ON
DANIEL BROWN

CODE:
DIGITAL
ENVIRONMENTS

3.18 *Dandelion*
Sennep and Yoke
Created using Processing,
this novel program explores
a physical way of interacting
with the environment. Virtual
dandelion seeds are blown
across the screen with a
hair dryer.

BOIDS

In the late 1980s, computer
scientist Craig Reynolds developed
algorithmic steering behaviors
for animated characters. These
behaviors allowed individual
elements to navigate their digital
environments in a "lifelike"
manner with strategies for fleeing,
wandering, arriving, pursuing,
evading, and so on. By building
a system of multiple characters
that steer themselves according
to a simple set of rules, surprising
levels of complexity emerge. The
most famous example is Reynolds's
"boids" model for "flocking/
swarming" behavior. This model of
behavior has been re-applied by
designers and artists to develop
swarms of characters that display
the kind of group behavior
displayed in the flocking and
steering activities of groups of fish
or birds.

ENVIRONMENTAL FORCES: GRAVITY, ELASTICITY

In addition to creating patterns of individual and group behavior movements and interactions of individual objects, code can also define the characteristics of the environment in which these objects move. Virtual, digital forces that replicate the physical properties of the natural environment, such as wind, friction, or gravity, can enhance the digital environment and affect the movement and motion of all the objects within. Simulation of forces that replicate "wind" within the screen world, can, for example, mean that graphics and pieces of typography are gracefully blown across the screen like leaves in a breeze. Adding or making changes to environmental factors (e.g., the values that alter the attributes of heaviness or lightness) changes the nature of the virtual scene and can determine whether objects on screen appear as if they are in air, in water, or in outer space. Changing the amount of computational "gravity" within a scene, for example, will affect the speed and movement of objects towards the "ground."

See Code section: Friction and Damping (page 89) & Gravity (page 90).

By adding behavioral and environmental qualities to the screen, code can transform the objects within a programmed environment so they act like living digital creatures, subject to change over time and able to live, grow, move, and even self-replicate. Digitally created objects can create a range of visually fascinating environments that can either be self-generating, like garden or pond eco-systems, or be generated and informed by user interaction.

EXEMPLAR

Bibliotheque Design: Ollo

A visual identity created for Ollo, a digital telecom company, explores the potential of interactive code to form a key part of a design solution. As part of the brand development, the logo is imagined not as a fixed, static visual, but as a living, organic shape with its own visually dynamic properties. To fit alongside the brand concept "one line of communication," the Ollo logo is created as a single, dynamically flexible line that can be manipulated via a touch-based interaction, which encourages users to push and pull the shape on the screen. Interactive manipulation of the logo becomes a creative tool in building the visual identity, which allows the designer to create an infinite number of unique digital assets that can be integrated into the brand. Computationally created physical forces, such as elasticity and springiness, give the shape its playfully expressive characteristics, which reflect the personality and informality of the brand.

3.19

3.19 Ollo Bibliotheque Design
A soft, responsive logo created for Ollo and made to match the personality of the brand. The digital flexibility of the logotype creates a brand image that encourages playful interaction with the customers and is open to almost infinite visual variety.

NATURE AS
INSPIRATION

DRAWING
AS GROWTH

ORGANIC
SHAPES:
SPIRALS
AND WAVES

COMPLEX
MATHEMATICAL
MODELS

DIGITAL
ECO-SYSTEMS

**ENVIRONMENTAL
FORCES: GRAVITY,
ELASTICITY**

SPOTLIGHT ON
DANIEL BROWN

CODE:
DIGITAL
ENVIRONMENTS

Everywhere: Oasis

Oasis is a playful interactive environment, a self-contained, pond-like eco-system inhabited by digitally generated life forms. The interactive application populates the environment with a range of various digital organisms, each with its own characteristics, behaviors, and movements. Using code to enhance and create the behaviors of each creature, users can play with the environment by forming ponds of life forms from the sand on the surface. The movement and interaction of the digital creatures is fascinating for viewers who can explore and watch; it re-creates the child-like interest of peering into a virtual rock-pool.

Digitally created eco-systems possess a lightness, beauty, and uniqueness of shape that are not always mathematically or scientifically precise but are artistic interpretations of the organic forms. The shapes, colors, form, and movement echo the lightness and beauty of the real world. Living within the space of a screen or projection blends the real and virtual environments.

3.20

3.20 *Oasis* **Everyware**
Virtual computational life forms emerge in digital "rock pools."

SPOTLIGHT ON

Daniel Brown

Daniel Brown is a designer, programmer, and artist and one of a generation of pioneers exploring creative uses and applications of interactive technology. He has been at the forefront of digital and interactive design since he launched his playful, innovative web experiments, Noodlebox, in 1997.

Daniel's work combines cutting-edge technology and programming with an aesthetic sense that is inspired by the decorative lightness and freshness of natural shapes and forms. He has produced work for a wide range of fashion and luxury brands in addition to creating private and public installations.

Natural botanical beauty—especially the shapes, forms, and colors of butterflies and flowers—suffuses Daniel's work. Many of his pieces translate botanical forms into a digital environment—flowers and plants that grow and reproduce. Complex technological processes and generative algorithms are hidden behind the elegance of the final pieces so that viewers appreciate not the clever application of code, but the aesthetic beauty of the pieces themselves.

3.21

NATURE AS
INSPIRATION

DRAWING
AS GROWTH

ORGANIC
SHAPES:
SPIRALS
AND WAVES

COMPLEX
MATHEMATICAL
MODELS

DIGITAL
ECO-SYSTEMS

ENVIRONMENTAL
FORCES: GRAVITY,
ELASTICITY

**SPOTLIGHT ON
DANIEL BROWN**

CODE:
DIGITAL
ENVIRONMENTS

3.21 *On Growth and Form*
Daniel Brown
Commissioned by the University
of Dundee, this is a generative
artwork created in homage to
D'Arcy Thompson's pioneering
book *On Growth and Form*
(1917) for the D'Arcy Thompson
Zoology Museum. Inspired
by shapes and textures in the
museum's exhibits, the work
generates digital plants and
flowers that continually grow
and re-generate. This piece
forms a part of Daniel's ongoing
series of generative artworks,
in which botanical shapes and
forms are created from complex
algorithms and computational
processes.

3.22

**3.22 *Mulberry Love Blossoms*
Daniel Brown**
The Love Blossoms project commissioned by Mulberry offers users the opportunity to send unique, digitally generated flowers as a Valentine's gift. By selecting a seasonal Mulberry pattern, the user sends a seed that grows into a unique digital flower. Computational processes are used to create the shapes and forms of each flower and petal, meaning that no two are ever the same, and the experience for each recipient is unique. The combination of interactive media with elegant naturalistic forms creates a beautiful digital experience for the viewer and the recipient.

How did you become interested in designing and programming?
From an early age, I was always interested in all things visual and computers. If I wasn't playing with the computer, I would be drawing or painting and getting myself and everything around me messy. You might say it was somewhat inevitable, with a mathematician and musician mother, and a programmer and painter father. The timing, however, was interesting. Until the mid-90s, the only real outlet for a mixture of such skills was the computer game industry, which I did consider going into quite seriously. But then, by fortunate timing, digital media came along and required the exact mix that I had accidentally stumbled upon out of passion rather than anything else. I won't pretend it was a master plan.

Where do you look to find creative inspiration for your work: Who or what motivates and inspires you?
At the root of it all are two core things:
• a desire to create interactive experiences which allow the public to empower themselves creatively and culturally.
• a curiosity in seeing how computers can synthesize the aesthetic found in nature and everyday physical phenomena, and how they can further create new aesthetics that go beyond the boundaries of that reality.

NATURE AS INSPIRATION

DRAWING AS GROWTH

ORGANIC SHAPES: SPIRALS AND WAVES

COMPLEX MATHEMATICAL MODELS

DIGITAL ECO-SYSTEMS

ENVIRONMENTAL FORCES: GRAVITY, ELASTICITY

SPOTLIGHT ON DANIEL BROWN

CODE: DIGITAL ENVIRONMENTS

The idea of playful experimentation is clear especially in your early work. What role does "play" and experimentation have as part of your creative practice?

I think that very much came out of the fact that as a teenager I was interested in computer games and the "demo scene." I was interested in how web technology could be used to create a more game-like experience, and in pushing the performance to its limit. On a personal level, anyone who knows me will tell you that I don't take life too seriously and if I can make anything more fun than boring and trivial for me and my friends, I will do!

Why do you code? Do you think that there are specific qualities or characteristics of programming which open up creative opportunities?

Well, the simple answer is that since 2003 when I sustained a very serious spinal injury, I have been severely paralyzed. I can no longer hold a brush, or a pencil, a scalpel, or even Lego. My only creative outlet is in writing code—which I am still fortunately able to do by means of an adapted computer. The long answer is that I enjoy the challenge of programming; it keeps me thinking every day what can I do that I haven't done before. When I think of aesthetics and design, I like to imagine styles and looks that don't exist yet; that's what I try to invent. Pens and pencils can't help you with that.

Working on the intersection between technology and creativity involves quite separate (left-brain / right-brain) activities. How is writing code integrated into your creative process?

Personally I don't see a distinction. I remember my mother playing the piano when I was child and improvising. I remember her telling me that once you practice playing an instrument to a certain point, it almost becomes a part of you and your hands can instinctively connect the song in your head with the keys. I think it's the same thing for me to use technology. My brain works instinctively in tune with the creative possibilities; I don't think about it.

Nature, growth, and form is a strong theme in your work. Do you see a connection between the organic and the computational environments?

The very first work in my flowers series was actually meant to be a technical demonstration of a particular type of computer algorithm. It was only after the London Design Museum saw it and asked to put it on display that I thought much about it. It turned out to be one of the most popular works in the show, and I realized that digital flowers are a fantastic way of demonstrating computer power and mathematics to the public. It's a universal aesthetic that everyone can understand.

You have created a wide range of projects and design work. Is there a particular piece or project of which you are most proud?

I would say my flowers series. Seeing young children jumping up trying to catch them when projected on the wall, or elderly people look in wonder as they grow all around them. Again, it's a universal beauty. It touches humanity.

Do you have any word of advice to young designers / students starting to explore this field of creative technology?

I'm going to sound rather boring and archaic, but I would suggest that you start out by really understanding how a computer works, and how you use computer code to interact with one. If you go down the path of learning one particular package or system— Unity or Flash, say—that is good, but you will still never really understand the difference between that system's limitations and the near-limitless possibilities of computing itself. It's hard work—sorry—but it offers great rewards. Creating something that was previously unimaginable only yesterday gives a great feeling of accomplishment.

CODE: DIGITAL ENVIRONMENTS

Many forces from the real world can be computationally simulated in the digital environment by applying simple mathematical calculations to create shape and movement. The following section outlines some useful examples.

Sine Wave

Go to www.bloomsbury.com/richardson-data-driven, Chapter 3, and click on the project "Sine Wave."

A sine wave is a mathematically described curve, often used in trigonometry, which can be applied to draw curved lines or create smooth bouncing movement. A sine function uses an angle to create a number sequence: As the angle increases, the number sequence "bounces" between a minimum (-1) and maximum (+1) value.

```
sine(angle); // syntax example
sin(radians(90)); // outputs 1
sin(radians(270)); // outputs -1
```

In Processing, angles are expressed as "radians," rather than as degrees. The radians() function is used here to convert the angle from degrees into radians.

Multiplying the result by a larger number, a "magnitude" value, "magnifies" the numbers into a more usable range.

```
float magnitude = 20; // create a "magnify" value
sin(radians(90)) * magnitude; // outputs 20
sin(radians(270))* magnitude; // outputs -20
```

As the value of the angle steadily increases, the number created by the sine function "bounces" between a minimum and maximum value. The following code re-calculates the location of a circle on the y-axis by using a sine function to move the shape up and down.

```
float angle=0; // starting angle
void draw(){
    // a "bouncing" value between -20 and 20
    float ypos = sin(radians(angle))*20;
    ellipse (10, ypos, 10, 10); // draw circle
    angle++; // increase angle by 1
}
```

By adding a variable to move the object across the stage at the same time, a simple wave (bounce) motion is created.

```
float angle = 0;
float xpos = 10;
void draw( ) {
    float ypos = sin(radians(angle))*20;
    // draw ellipse with variables for x and y
    ellipse (xpos, ypos+50, 10, 10);
    angle++; // increase angle by 1
    xpos += 2; // increase xpos value
}
```

A sine wave can be used to move objects in a wave-like motion across the screen. Making adjustments to calculations, such as the rate at which the angle value increases or the magnitude number, alters the type of wave and motion produced.

NATURE AS
INSPIRATION

DRAWING
AS GROWTH

ORGANIC
SHAPES:
SPIRALS
AND WAVES

COMPLEX
MATHEMATICAL
MODELS

DIGITAL
ECO-SYSTEMS

ENVIRONMENTAL
FORCES: GRAVITY,
ELASTICITY

SPOTLIGHT ON
DANIEL BROWN

**CODE:
DIGITAL
ENVIRONMENTS**

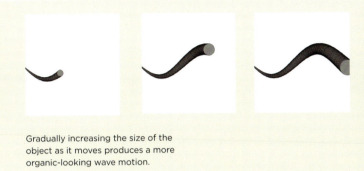

Gradually increasing the size of the
object as it moves produces a more
organic-looking wave motion.

TRY IT

Apply a sine function to the movement of a shape to "bounce"
the shape across the screen.
Try applying a sine function to change other variable values
applied to other properties of a shape, such as its size or color.

Environment and Forces

The movement and behavior of interactive objects can be
given added realism by adding computational simulations of
real-world forces such as friction, gravity, wind, and elasticity.

*Go to www.bloomsbury.com/richardson-data-driven, Chapter 3,
and click on the project "Inertia and Damping."*

Friction and Damping

The movements of objects in the real world are subject
to friction and other resistive forces, which make objects
gradually decelerate before stopping. Roll a ball across the
floor and it does not come to an immediate halt; instead, it
gradually slows down. This deceleration effect is achieved
mathematically by multiplying a "speed" value by a fraction.
Repeatedly multiplying a number by fractional value (e.g.,
0.5 or 0.9) slowly decreases ("dampens") its value and is a
good way to simulate a slowing-down effect. For example, if a
variable "speed" starts with a value of 100, multiplying by 0.5
will reduce the speed to 50% of its value each time.

```
float speed = 100;
speed = speed*0.5; //speed becomes 50
speed = speed*0.5; //speed becomes 25
speed = speed*0.5; //speed becomes 12.5
speed = speed*0.5; //speed becomes 6.25
speed = speed*0.5; //speed becomes 3.125
```

Halving the values each time means that the rate change
between the numbers gradually decreases. Mapping this
change visually creates a slowing-down effect.

Altering the fraction value changes the rate of movement. In
the following example, the speed value, used to change the x
location of the shape, is continually multiplied by 0.9, which
has the effect of "damping" the speed and decelerating the
shape's movement.

```
// create starting variables for speed and x location
float speed = 5;
float xpos = 10;
void draw( ) {
    speed = speed*0.9; // "dampen" the speed
    xpos = xpos + speed; // update the shape location
    ellipse (xpos, 50, 10, 10); // draw shape
}
```

Using a fractional number value to "dampen" the horizontal
speed of an object can be used to create an effect in which
an object gradually slows down as it nears a target. In the
following example, a circle is moved towards a fixed point,
gradually decelerating as it does so.

During the looped "draw" section of the code, the distance between the object's x location (xpos) and its target point (targetX) is re-calculated. This value represents the total distance between the ball and its end destination, and is stored as the variable ("distanceToMove"). Instead of moving the circle to its target in one single leap, a "damping" value is used to move the circle a fraction of the total distance required.

As this process is repeated, the distance between the ball and its target becomes smaller and the fractions become smaller, having the effect of slowing the object gradually to a halt.

```
float damping = 0.1;
float targetX = 90; // target x location to aim for
float xpos = 10; // starting x location

void draw( ){
  background (0);
   // find how far to move
  float distanceToMove = targetX–xpos;
   // move a fraction of distance
  xpos = xpos + (distanceToMove * damping);
  ellipse (xpos, 50, 10, 10);
}
```

An object gradually slows down to a halt.

TRY IT

Re-create the examples above.
Try applying "damping" to both movement on the x and y axis at the same time.

Gravity

Go to www.bloomsbury.com/richardson-data-driven, Chapter 3, and click on the project "Gravity."

Computational "gravity" is represented in code as a number, which is continually added to a speed value and steadily increases the movement of an object. Speed begins at 0, but as the gravity value is added to it over and again, quickly gathers momentum.

```
float gravity = 0.3; // a constant gravity value
// use gravity to increase speed
speed = speed + gravity;
// change y location using speed
ypos = ypos + speed;
ellipse (10, ypos, 5, 5); // draw object
```

By looping this process, a programmer creates the effect of an object falling with gravitational force:

```
float gravity = 0.1; // a set value
float speed = 0; // a changing value that increases
// the starting y location of the ball
float ypos =0;

void draw( ){
  // gradually increase the speed
  speed = speed + gravity;
  // update the y location of the object
  ypos = ypos + speed;
  ellipse(10, ypos, 5, 5); // draw the ball
}
```

A falling shape subject to computational gravity increases speed as it nears the ground.

Bounce

Go to www.bloomsbury.com/richardson-data-driven, Chapter 3, and click on the project "Bounce."

Gravity makes a shape drop and fall off the edge of the screen. "Bounce" can be added by reversing the speed of the object when it hits the "ground." Reversing the speed reverses the direction of movement. To reverse the speed value, multiply it by a negative number. Multiplying anything by -1 will switch it from a positive to a negative, or from a negative to a positive number:

```
 10 * -1 = -10;
-10 * -1 = 10;
```

Multiplying speed by a negative number therefore has the effect of reversing the direction of an object, creating a "bounce" effect. Using -0.95 rather than -1 "dampens" the speed, causing the object to lose a little momentum with each "bounce."

```
// reverse direction and lose energy
speed = speed * -0.95;
```

The "bounce" effect needs to be triggered at a certain point (i.e., when the ball falls too far or "hits the ground"). In code terms, this means triggering the reverse in speed when the y location of the object has hit, or fallen below, the "ground level" on the screen. An "if" statement is used within the draw() section to continually check the y location of the object as it falls. If the ball hits, or falls beyond the bottom edge of the screen, then the speed is reversed and the ball bounces.

```
if (ypos>height) {
    speed = speed * -0.95;
}
```

Wind

Go to www.bloomsbury.com/richardson-data-driven, Chapter 3, and click on the project "Wind."

Just as gravity is a number that is used to affect the y location of an object, so computational "wind" can be generated by using a number to affect the x location of an object and push it sideways. Adding a force to alter sideways movement can be used to simulate a "breeze" blowing across the screen.

```
float wind = 0.4;
xpos = xpos + wind;
ellipse (xpos, 100, 50, 50);
```

The combined effects of the gravity and wind forces give the digital environment properties that begin to simulate the behaviors in a natural physical eco-system. Digital objects come to life, moving in simple but effectively realistic ways.

```
float speed = 0;
float gravity = 0.3;
float wind = 0.4;
float ypos = 0;
float xpos = 10;

void draw() {
    speed = speed + gravity; // increase speed
    ypos = ypos + speed; // move ball's y position
    xpos = xpos + wind; // move ball's x position
    ellipse (xpos, ypos, 10, 10); // draw ball
    // reverse speed when the ball reaches bottom of
    screen
    if (ypos>height) {
        speed = speed*-0.95;
    }
}
```

TRY IT

Create an object that falls using gravity.
Try different values of gravity to alter the effect.
Allow the shape to "bounce" when it hits the edge of the screen.

TRY IT

Add a variable that affects the amount of sideways motion of an object ("wind").
Experiment with different values for this variable.

An example shape moved by computational forces of "gravity" and "wind." Gravity increases the speed of the shape as it moves toward the ground. When it reaches the base of the screen, the speed is reversed to "bounce" the shape. An additional "wind" force moves the object sideways as it falls.

Springs and Elastics

Go to www.bloomsbury.com/richardson-data-driven, Chapter 3, and click on the project "Elasticity."

Forces of elasticity create movements that give objects a lively, spring-like behavior. The movement of a spring is replicated in code using a standard calculation used to model this kind of elastic force.

```
spring force = stiffness * distance stretched;
```

Stiffness represents how "bouncy" the spring is; the distance stretched could be the distance between a graphic and its intended rest location. Once calculated, spring force is added to change the movement of an object. Damping is applied to make sure the spring gradually slows down to a stop. Spring forces could be applied to the movement of an object in the following way:

```
// create starting variables
float stiffness = 0.1; // a constant value
// a constant value to dampen the force
float damping = 0.9;

float targetX = 80; // location to "spring" to
float xpos;
float speed;
void draw( ){
    // calculate spring force
    float spring_force = stiffness * (targetX-xpos);
    // add force to speed
    speed = speed + spring_force;
    // apply damping
    speed = speed * damping;
    xpos = xpos + speed;
    ellipse (xpos, 50, 20, 20)
}
```

This type of bouncy spring force can be especially effective when moving shapes to a destination, giving the movement an extra level of "vitality." It can also give graphics an increased element of physicality when used to change the size of a shape: a wobbly kind of squash-and-stretch effect.

TRY IT

Re-create the example here.
Experiment with different settings to adjust the spring movement.

Objects and Groups

Go to www.bloomsbury.com/richardson-data-driven, Chapter 3, and click on the project "OOP."

The above are examples in which a single shape (a ball) is moved by values that simulate forces of gravity and wind. This works fine for a single shape, but what if you wanted to create many more similarly moving objects—for example, as particles or leaves blown by the breeze?

Repeating the same processes to create hundreds of similar moving shapes would require new sets of variables and calculations for every new shape, and would quickly get very complicated. A more useful and efficient way to do this would be to use object oriented processes and to create a generic behavior as a "class."

A Programming "Class"

In programming, a "class" is a block of code that acts as a template (blueprint) from which lots of individual objects can be created. The class defines the generic properties and behaviors of each object. When individual objects are created, they inherit the same generic properties and behaviors, but each object may have different values for certain properties (e.g., be a different size or color value). Creating a class allows the programmer to re-create and re-produce lots of similar objects that have a shared generic behavior and look.

The "Car" Class Example

A class is a template that is used to create lots of similar objects. They can be as simple or as complex as required.

Classes are written as collections of variables and functions that define the properties (characteristics) and methods (behaviors) of an object. Every instance of the class inherits the same set of properties and behaviors. For example, think of a car. Every car shares the same general properties (they each have doors, engine, gears, etc.) and behaviors (they can accelerate, turn, brake). When it is built, each car "object" has individual differences (color, make, model); they may be different shapes and sizes, but each comes from the same

generic template. This is the same for objects created by a class: They share the same template but each has individual qualities.

In our example, the "car" class would be written to define the generic properties and functions of a car as follows:

```
class Car {
    // define properties of the car
    float engineSize;
    int numberOfDoors;
    float maxSpeed;

    // define the "constructor"* to create a car
    Car (float ms) {
        maxSpeed = ms;
    }

    // define some behaviors:functions of the car
    void changeSpeed ( ) {
        // add functions here
    }

    void changeDirection ( ) {
        // add functions here
    }
}
```

Once the class has been written, individual instances (objects) can be created from it. New cars can be created from the car class by creating a "new" instance that calls the constructor function written into the class. In this example, a new car is constructed and sets the maxSpeed value of each new car instance:

```
// a new "car" instance
Car car1 = new Car (120);
// another new "car" instance
Car car2 = new Car (200);
```

TIP: The "constructor" function is a function that shares the same name as the class and is automatically called when the class is used. The constructor function is used to set the specific values to properties of the class. In this example, when the class is used the maxSpeed of each individual car is defined.

Once instances of the class have been created, the properties and functions written in the "template" class can be accessed using "dot" notation. For example, each car that has been created (car1, car2) can set or change its engineSize property as follows:

```
car1.engineSize = 200;
car2.engineSize = car1.engineSize + 20;
```

Similarly, they can call the changeSpeed() or changeDirection() functions.

```
car1.changeSpeed();
car2.changeDirection();
```

A Class to Create Multiple Shapes

Go to www.bloomsbury.com/richardson-data-driven, Chapter 3, and click on the project "OOP Shapes."

In a previous example, a single shape was moved by a gravity value. The movement of the shape was generated using three variables:

```
float gravity = 0.1;
float speed = 0;
float ypos = 0;
```

The main program looped three main instructions: increase the speed, update the location, and draw the shape.

```
// increase the speed
speed = speed + gravity;
// update the location of the object
ypos = ypos + speed;
// draw the shape
ellipse(10, ypos, 5, 5);
```

These variables and the instructions can be used as the basis for a generic circle "class" that can be used as a template for creating loads of similar falling circle shapes. The example circle class can include variables to control the object's gravity, speed, and y position, and functions to increase its speed, update its location, and draw the shape. The following code is an example starting point for creating this type of re-usable circle class.

```
class Circle {
    // name the properties
    float speed;
    float ypos;
    float gravity;

    // set the "constructor" to set the gravity and y
    position each instance
    Circle (float g, float y) {
        gravity = g;
        ypos = y;
    }

    // create simple functions: re-locate the circle
    void updateSpeedAndLocation ( ) {
        speed = speed + gravity;
        ypos = ypos + speed;
    }

    // draw the circle
    void drawShape( ) {
        ellipse(10, ypos, 5, 5);
    }
}
```

Once created, the circle class can be used to create lots of new individual instances, each with its own starting gravity and ypos values (as defined in the "constructor" function).

NATURE AS INSPIRATION

DRAWING AS GROWTH

ORGANIC SHAPES: SPIRALS AND WAVES

COMPLEX MATHEMATICAL MODELS

DIGITAL ECO-SYSTEMS

ENVIRONMENTAL FORCES: GRAVITY, ELASTICITY

SPOTLIGHT ON DANIEL BROWN

CODE: DIGITAL ENVIRONMENTS

```
// create a new circle with a gravity of 0.1 and y
position of 10
Circle c1 = new Circle (0.1, 10);
// create a new circle with a gravity of 0.2 and y
position of 20
Circle c2 = new Circle (0.2, 20);
```

Defining different gravity and ypos values makes each circle start at a different height and fall at a different rate. Both of the new circle instances ("c1" and "c2") can now call the functions written into the class used to move and draw each shape on the screen:

```
c1.updateSpeedAndLocation();
c1.drawShape();
c2.updateSpeedAndLocation();
c2.drawShape();
```

This simple example shows how a class structure is used to create re-usable objects and behaviors. Assigning individual values to the properties of each instance gives each object its own unique identity. Once the basic structure has been created, more complexity can be added by, for example, adding more variables (e.g., to specify the size or x location of each individual circle), or by adding extra functions, such as "bounce."

Object oriented programming allows groups of objects to be created with the same generic behavior.

Filling an array can populate the screen with objects with similar behaviors. Individual instances of each object have slight differences that change attributes such as their size, starting location, or speed of movement.

TRY IT

Create a sample "circle" class to make a shape affected by gravity. Create two or three circle instances and call the functions to draw and move them.
Add extra variables to the class to alter the x location and size of each instance.
Add a "bounce" function to react when a circle hits the ground.

Once the class has been created, an array can be created to hold and store lots of instances all together. This provides a quick way to create and access tens or hundreds of object instances at once. The following example creates a list ("circleList") that is able to hold up to 10 circle instances.

```
Circle [ ] circleList = new Circle [10];
```

A "for" loop is used to populate the list with Circle objects, giving each instance a different gravity and ypos value:

```
for (int i=0; i<circleList.length; i++) {
    circleList[i] = new Circle (random (0.7), i*10);
}
```

Another "for" loop can then be used to cycle through the list and call the updateSpeedAndLocation() and drawShape functions to each circle instance in turn:

```
for (int i=0; i<circleList.length; i++) {
    circleList[i].updateSpeedAndLocation( );
    circleList[i].drawShape( );
}
```

TIP: There are lots of additional code-based libraries available which have been specifically designed to simulate the forces of the physical world in more complex ways (bounce, gravity) both in 2D and 3D. Processing libraries that do this, such as "Box2D for Processing," are listed on the website: https://processing.org/reference/libraries/

95

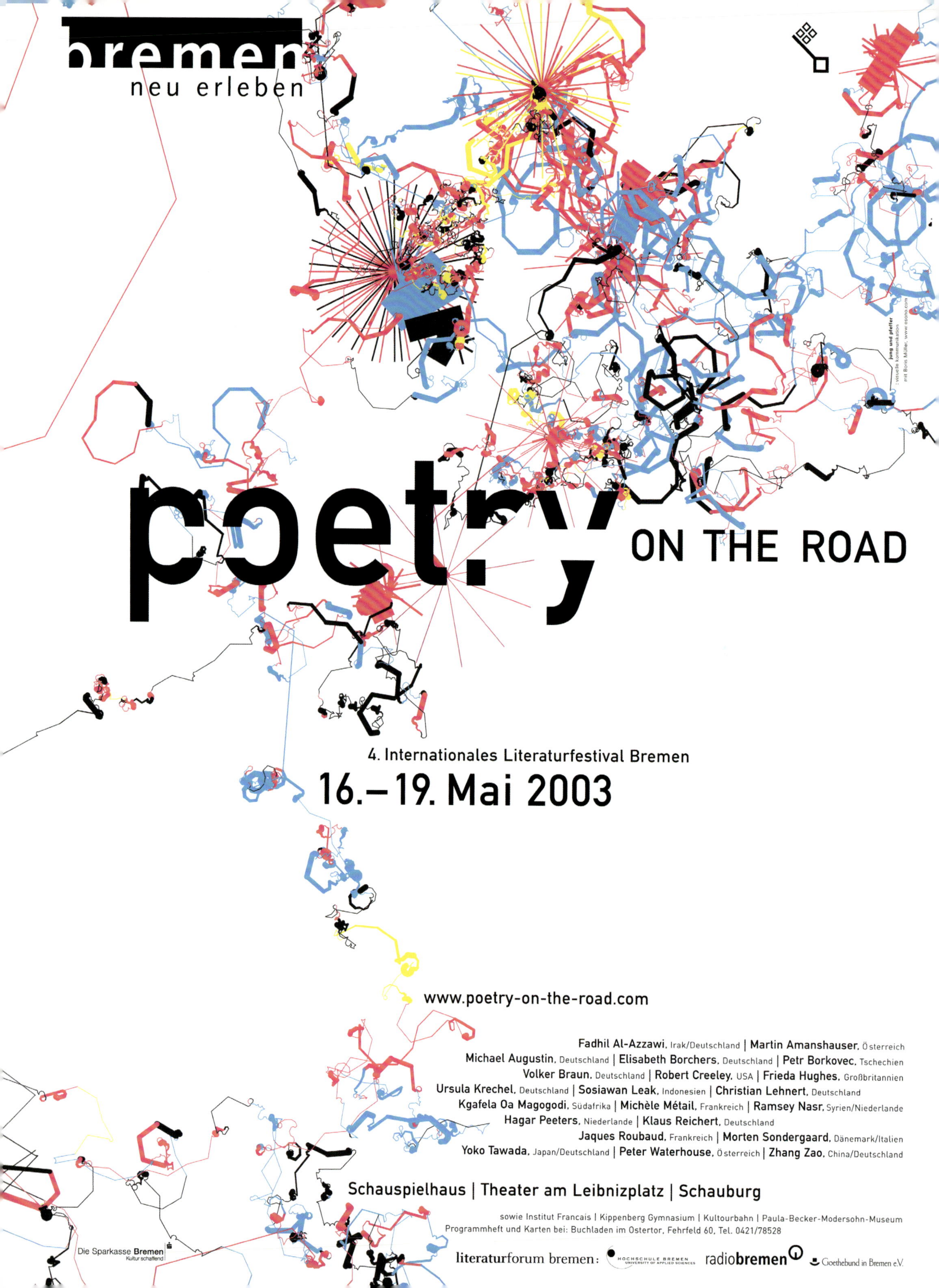

bremen
neu erleben

poetry ON THE ROAD

4. Internationales Literaturfestival Bremen
16.–19. Mai 2003

www.poetry-on-the-road.com

Fadhil Al-Azzawi, Irak/Deutschland | Martin Amanshauser, Österreich
Michael Augustin, Deutschland | Elisabeth Borchers, Deutschland | Petr Borkovec, Tschechien
Volker Braun, Deutschland | Robert Creeley, USA | Frieda Hughes, Großbritannien
Ursula Krechel, Deutschland | Sosiawan Leak, Indonesien | Christian Lehnert, Deutschland
Kgafela Oa Magogodi, Südafrika | Michèle Métail, Frankreich | Ramsey Nasr, Syrien/Niederlande
Hagar Peeters, Niederlande | Klaus Reichert, Deutschland
Jaques Roubaud, Frankreich | Morten Sondergaard, Dänemark/Italien
Yoko Tawada, Japan/Deutschland | Peter Waterhouse, Österreich | Zhang Zao, China/Deutschland

Schauspielhaus | Theater am Leibnizplatz | Schauburg

sowie Institut Francais | Kippenberg Gymnasium | Kultourbahn | Paula-Becker-Modersohn-Museum
Programmheft und Karten bei: Buchladen im Ostertor, Fehrfeld 60, Tel. 0421/78528

Die Sparkasse Bremen
Kultur schaffend

literaturforum bremen : HOCHSCHULE BREMEN UNIVERSITY OF APPLIED SCIENCES   radiobremen   Goethebund in Bremen e.V.

CHAPTER FOUR
DYNAMIC TYPOGRAPHY

"Typography needs to be audible.
Typography needs to be felt.
Typography needs to be experienced."
Helmut Schmid

FORM AND CONTENT

Typography has played a critical role in visual communication and forms a key part of graphic design practice. From the earliest pioneers in the early twentieth century right up to the present day, graphic designers have experimented with the creative possibilities of type and letterforms as a mode of visual communication.

The changing technological landscape has opened up a host of creative opportunities for designers to experiment and explore ways of playing with the form and look of letters and fonts. Pixelated layers in a bitmap document, points and paths in a vector file, objects in a 3D landscape, and an array of filters effects: all allow digital text to be transformed and reconfigured in a range of different ways. The concept of "text as image" is common; software tools allow and encourage visual playfulness with words and letters as they are stretched, combined, and layered.

In addition to changing the aesthetics of typography, digital technology has also changed the way in which type and words are read. Digital media has shifted the concept of text from that of a fixed and permanent set of printed words toward a digital data source whose content and form can be read, re-read, and manipulated. In the digital world, words are not fixed to a page; they exist in an environment in which form and content is subject to alteration.

Designers are able to use code to creatively re-imagine the shape and content of text. Using programming code, digital text can be manipulated either as shape data—points, lines, and curves that create dynamic, animated visuals as letterforms—or as content—for example, text files of digital information, novels, books, and poems—whose content is used to create and generate graphics. This chapter will give an overview of the ways in which digital data can be used to create and manipulate text and typography—both as form and as content.

See Code section: Anatomy of Text as Data (page 120).

Type as form

Programming rules and structures can be creatively applied to dynamically transform and combine individual pieces of text or to manipulate their forms. They can be applied either to manipulate existing fonts and letterforms or to create new, computationally generated shapes. Unlike "closed" software-driven procedures, limited to a pre-set range of image manipulation techniques (filters, warping, etc.), programming methods open up the creative possibilities of working with the details of type, allowing designers to play and experiment with the fundamental visual attributes of typographic shapes and to produce unique and original variations of the form.

4.2

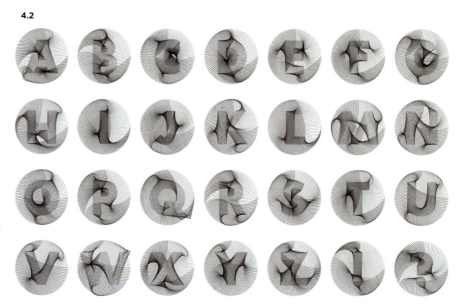

FORM AND
CONTENT

MOVEMENT
AND
INTERACTIVE
TYPE

TEXT
AS DATA
SOURCE

EXTERNAL
DATA

SPOTLIGHT ON
ARIEL MALKA

CODE:
COMPUTATIONAL
TYPOGRAPHY

Rules and Transformations

Applying programming functions to a letter or word shape encourages the designer to fundamentally re-think and re-imagine its typographic form, structure, and composition to rebuild digital letters. Programming rules can be used to apply mathematical transformations that visually re-calculate a shape in a numerically predictable and controllable way. Code that systematically or randomly repeats, scales, transforms, moves, or otherwise manipulates parts of or entire letters can create unique compositions and letters. Individual letter shapes can be transformed and combined into rhythmic patterns by repeatedly recalculating or deconstructing the position or shape of a letter.

4.2 *Code-Type* **Kyuha Shim**
An example piece from Kyuha Shim's "Code and Type" project (previous page), which uses computational processes to produce digital letterforms. The rules of code allow shapes to be repeated and transformed and the repetition of a rotating line creates a unique set of code-based letters.

EXEMPLAR

Ricard Marxer: Caligraft

Caligraft is an experimental project that takes inspiration from traditional calligraphy (the art of decorative writing) and uses programming to generate digital "calligraphic" letterforms. Code is used to dynamically re-interpret letters in a variety of ways, abstracting the original shapes into a series of animated forms, each of which has its own kind of distinctive character and style. Digital strokes and lines that animate and generate the letters reflect the hand-drawn aesthetic of traditional calligraphy in a uniquely digital way. The project works as a series of playful online experiments that explore ways of creating digitally "handmade" work using code.

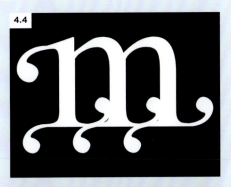

4.4 *Caligraft* **Ricard Marxer**
Other experiments from the Caligraft project combine letter shapes according to well-defined generative rules.

4.3 *Caligraft* **Ricard Marxer**
Ricard Marxer's Caligraft project uses a self-made generative system to play with re-creating letters. The "sketches" animate and draw characters in a fluid way. A series of experiments explore different rules for modifying letter shapes. Each experiment is a visual representation of a wider design process in which a set of rules and functions has been systematically applied to generate the work.

Shape paths and points

Code transforms words and letters into digitally pliable shapes. Individual co-ordinate points and paths describing and defining the points and curves of a letter shape can be changed using code to dynamically alter its visual appearance. Designers can use programming functions to visually pull letter shapes apart. When subject to computational rules and forces (such as recursion, repetition, physical movement, randomness), the strokes and lines, points and curves of a letter shape can re-generate into typographic forms and become graphics either for screen or print.

Programming methods used to deconstruct type and letter shapes encourage a kind of visual inventiveness that can develop new versions of the letter shapes. The outline paths and curves of a letter can be used as motion guides along which objects animate, visually re-inventing the letter shape as a series of dynamic moving lines. Individual points of a single letter shape can be used as co-ordinates for "seeding" points from which digital lines organically grow and reproduce or even as "magnetic" points towards and around which other graphics, lines, shapes, and colors gravitate and interact.

4.5

FORM AND
CONTENT

MOVEMENT
AND
INTERACTIVE
TYPE

TEXT
AS DATA
SOURCE

EXTERNAL
DATA

SPOTLIGHT ON
ARIEL MALKA

CODE:
COMPUTATIONAL
TYPOGRAPHY

Letter shapes from date

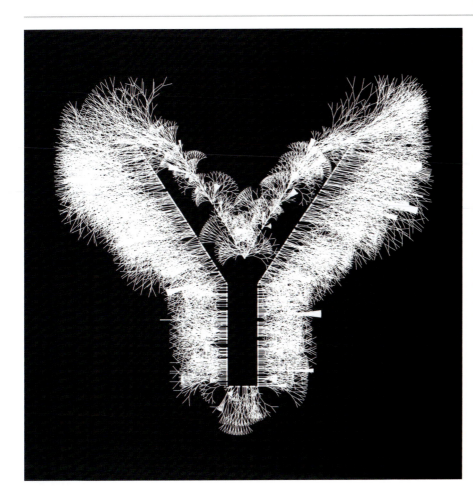

A range of external data sources can also modify the co-ordinate points and values of a letter. For instance, mouse movements, audio, or a sequence of key presses can be captured and applied as information to change the visual details of a letter shape. The size, shape, or color of typography can be generated as a visual response to external audio files from, for example, speech or a bird song. Linking a typographic shape with a data source opens up new ways of expressing and creating typographic experiences. Words become a visual expression of a specific experience or idea. Unique computational typefaces can be created that visually represent a specific data set or series of actions captured and "frozen" into a visual format.

4.5 Yeohyun Ahn
Examples of work from Yeohyun Ahn, a typographer and interactive visual designer, who explores the link between art, design, and typography. These experimental pieces of typography use Processing and Ricard Marxer's Geomerative library to re-imagine letterforms as code-generated environments.

EXEMPLAR

Reza Ali mis.shap.en.ness

Reza Ali is a programmer and designer whose research has led him to explore the visual possibilities of applying code to dynamically generate shape and form. By connecting data sources and computationally generated physical forces into a framework for creating shapes and images, he has been able to generate an interesting body of experimental shapes. Seeing typography as a pliable computational form whose shape can be sculpted and changed in response to external forces and data, Reza has experimented with creating "generative" typography: letter shapes that are responsive to built-in particle systems as well as external audio files.

The results, documented on his blog, are a series of wonderfully colorful, fluid, typographic forms with uniquely changeable qualities; they work either as static or animated graphics. The experiments highlight how, having abstracted the letter shapes into a series of individual colors and points and created a connection with the data (e.g., an audio file), Reza continues to experiment by changing parameters in order to get a range of different results. Reza applies and re-uses simple programmed forces (e.g., springs and particles) to affect the color and shape of the letters. Simple, subtle changes of these parameters and values yield a range of different visuals generated from one concept.

4.6

4.6 *mis.shap.en.ness*
Reza Ali
The outlines of letters are transformed into flexible shapes by applying code-generated particles that move and fall, distorting the words as they "drip" down the screen.

FORM AND
CONTENT

MOVEMENT
AND
INTERACTIVE
TYPE

TEXT
AS DATA
SOURCE

EXTERNAL
DATA

SPOTLIGHT ON
ARIEL MALKA

CODE:
COMPUTATIONAL
TYPOGRAPHY

4.7

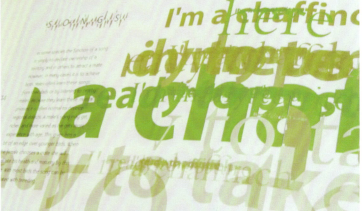

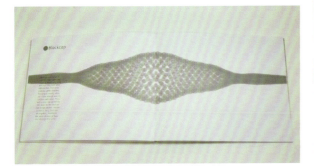

**4.7 See the sounds of nature
Elena Kalaydzhieva**

In this example of experimental design work, the typography is generated in response to the audio files of bird song recorded during the dawn chorus. Processing is used to visualize each of the songs of the birds through graphical sound waves and manipulating the typography. The final printed outcome includes the images created from the Processing application.

MOVEMENT AND INTERACTIVE TYPE

Code not only generates new letter shapes and forms but can also be used to create animated and "reactive" typographic experiences: letters that move in response to user interaction. Programming methods can divide and sub-divide the formal structure of a line or paragraph of text into a string of individual words, letters, or points. Rigid rows of text can be transformed into flexible, free-floating objects, subject to internally or externally generated interactive rules and forces. Freeing letters from their original formatting allows the typography to be playfully and interactively animated. Individual letters become kinetic, graphical objects whose positions, points, and contours can be manipulated.

See Code section: Using Variables With Text (page 121).

The creative application of programming allows words to jump from the page into an interactive environment: Mouse movement, user gesture, sound input, and so on can be used to dynamically twist and manipulate typography into interactively flexible shapes and movements, sending them spinning, rotating, or dancing on the screen, blown by virtual winds of user-generated interaction. Computational rules can make digital typography interactive, allowing viewers to engage with content in new ways.

See Code section: Adding Animation: Jiggle, Rotate (page 124).

EXEMPLAR

Nanika (Andreas Müller): For All Seasons app

4.8

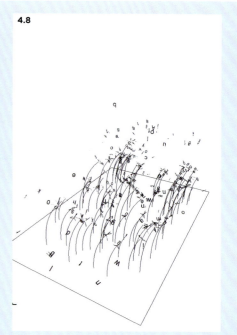

The For All Seasons app is a version of a 2005 interactive typographic piece created by Andreas Müller. The work is an experimental and playful exploration of interactive typography. It is divided into four passages of text, each describing a memory associated with a season of the year. In each case, the letters and words from the passage transform into a corresponding interactive environment.

The words transform into dandelion seeds that get blown in the wind (spring), swimming fish (summer), piles of fallen leaves (autumn), and falling snowflakes (winter). Users are able to explore and interact with each environment, causing the letters to get blown gracefully across the screen, swim, or fall gently on a tree (as snow). The organic, naturalistic movement of the letters mirrors the digital environment they are in, creating an engaging, playful, and poetic association with each passage of text.

Each screen is a new environment. The letters become the objects in the environment (seeds, fish, leaves, snow) that are moved by naturalistic forces of the virtual world. The project is a good example of the affinity between the organic and digital environment, as the movement of the programmed objects takes inspiration from and beautifully mirrors that found in the natural world.

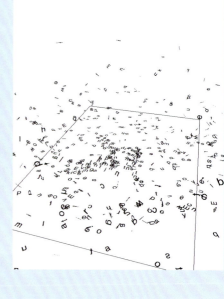

FORM AND
CONTENT

**MOVEMENT
AND
INTERACTIVE
TYPE**

TEXT
AS DATA
SOURCE

EXTERNAL
DATA

SPOTLIGHT ON
ARIEL MALKA

CODE:
COMPUTATIONAL
TYPOGRAPHY

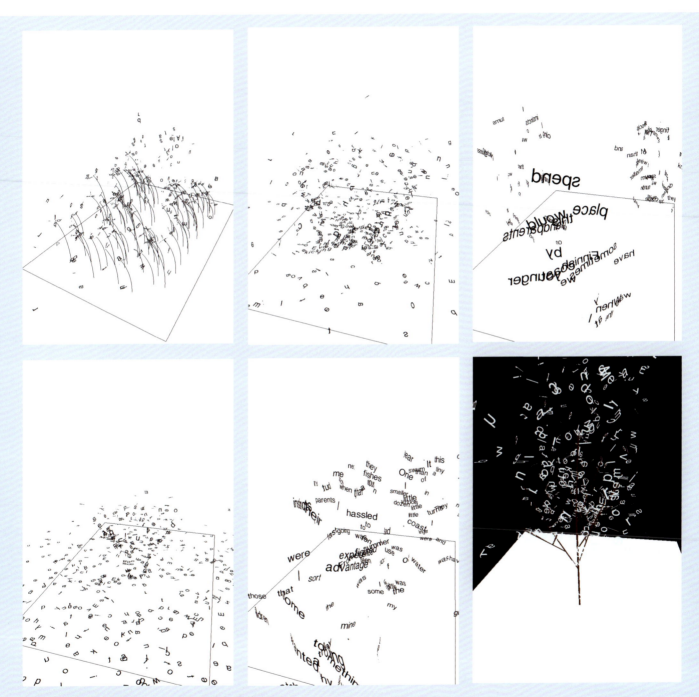

4.8 *For All Seasons* Nanika
A playful use of typography in which emotions are explored through interactive recollections of each of the seasons. Each natural environment features letters and words that seem to organically move as computational rules guide them.

EXEMPLAR

Born **Magazine**

An early experiment in the use of digital media to create engaging interactive text-experiences, *Born* (bornmagazine.org) is/was a experimental collaborative project bringing together designers, artists, and writers to generate interactive, online poems and explore the poetic qualities of interactive and moving typography.

Born provided a place for digital designers, artists, and writers to collaborate to create visually rich interactive poems and stories. A combination of graphics programming and writing helped to create an open area for exploring and pushing the boundaries of digitally interactive ways of experiencing and reading text.

4.9

FORM AND
CONTENT

**MOVEMENT
AND
INTERACTIVE
TYPE**

TEXT
AS DATA
SOURCE

EXTERNAL
DATA

SPOTLIGHT ON
ARIEL MALKA

CODE:
COMPUTATIONAL
TYPOGRAPHY

4.9

4.9 *Zoology* **Sasha West
(author) and Ernesto Lavandera
(artist)**
Screen shots from the project
published in the online magazine
Born.

4.10

4.10 *Walking Together What
Remains* **Chris Green (author)
and Erik Natzke (artist)**
Screen shots from the project
published in the online magazine
Born.

Moving and interactive typography gives digital letters new life and character. Code makes animated letterforms interactive and changeable; programmers can shift the letterforms' content according to user input and interaction and allow users to read and experience words in a uniquely interactive and digital way. Creating interactive environments of text can enliven user engagement with the content and change the way the words are understood. Reading becomes a playful, poetic experience in which the users can construct meanings from their own explorations of the words. The arrival of hand-held screens and tablets brings the experience of reading digital text even closer to that of reading a physical book and presents more opportunities for creating rich, interactive content.

See Code section: Letters as Dynamic Objects (page 124).

FORM AND
CONTENT

MOVEMENT
AND
INTERACTIVE
TYPE

TEXT
AS DATA
SOURCE

EXTERNAL
DATA

SPOTLIGHT ON
ARIEL MALKA

CODE:
COMPUTATIONAL
TYPOGRAPHY

4.11

4.11 *Wordscapes* **Peter Cho**
Peter Cho's interactive
typography work represents
an exploration of the creative
possibilities of computational
interactive text. Wordscapes
is a collection of twenty-six
playful interactive typographic
landscapes.

TEXT AS DATA SOURCE

Code allows designers to access and use text as an important data source that can be visually interpreted. Using the characteristics of a text source as information to drive and direct the style and format of the visuals establishes a relationship between the content and its graphical treatment. Code can "mine" the details of text, reveal hidden details (word count, word frequency, letter count, line length, word length, the relationships between words, etc.), translating them into number values and applying them to define visual elements (color, shape, geometry, or rotation). Using code in this way opens up opportunities to delve into the structure and content of words, "dig below" surface meaning, reveal and visualize "hidden" patterns and relationships within the content. Artists and designers are able to generate their own new visual associations between the text and image, transforming and visualizing selected attributes of the text and creating new visual expressions of the words.

See Code section: Text as Data: Load Strings (page 126).

Abstracting text

The idea of transforming text into a set of visual attributes may seem an abstract or difficult concept. However, like much of the information used in programming code, the values and attributes of a piece of text are processed and understood by the computer as numbers. Number values form a highly significant part of any programming code; they set and define the visual details of every object. Numbers in code are transformative values: flexible pieces of data that can be used to define and change reams of visual elements and attributes. Numbers can define color, shape, texture, or movement. For designers using code, numbers provide a useful, direct way to change and manipulate graphics. The idea that a piece of writing can be represented in a number format is therefore key to understanding how text can be visualized in a graphical format. It opens up a vista of creative design work.

Text data can be derived directly from user input or from data saved and input from an external file. Sources of letter and word information can be computationally analyzed, abstracted, and transformed to generate unique sets of graphics. A simple example relates to how graphics can be generated from keyboard input.

EXEMPLAR

Boris Müller: Poetry on the Road

Poetry on the Road is an ongoing experimental visual design project based around an annual literature festival held in Bremen, Germany. Each year since 2002, the designer Boris Müller has been commissioned to create a visual theme that reflects the work of the writers featured in the festival.

The graphical challenge, to represent a diverse range of writing in a visually coherent manner, is an interesting one, which Boris solves by using code as a way of visualizing the literature. A bespoke programming system is created that turns the text into images; each graphic directly represents of a particular piece of writing.

Even though the basic concept remains the same, each new programming system is designed to draw and visualize words in a different way, creating new connections and generating a fascinating range of graphical and interactive work. Each version of the project creates new visual interpretations of the poems because different methods of transforming words into images are explored. Connections between the content of a poem and the graphics are made in a variety of interesting ways, each of which produces a unique visual outcome.

FORM AND
CONTENT

MOVEMENT
AND
INTERACTIVE
TYPE

**TEXT
AS DATA
SOURCE**

EXTERNAL
DATA

SPOTLIGHT ON
ARIEL MALKA

CODE:
COMPUTATIONAL
TYPOGRAPHY

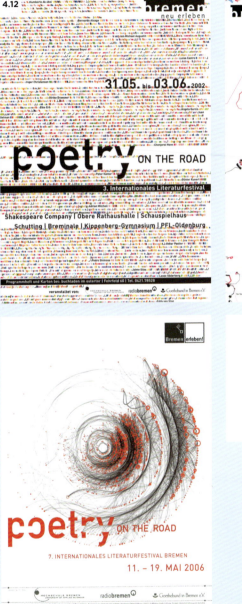

The attributes of the words and letters in each poem are deconstructed and used to create abstract shapes whose visual attributes (color, shape, position, direction, etc.) are determined by the number values and the characteristics found within the words themselves (e.g., letter count, word frequency, and size). By this method, individual letters are abstracted into colored boxes and lines; common words are found, made larger, and connected together; and entire poems are drawn as a "particle" field of words with its own set of forces. Other experiments push further at the visual connections between word and image: Poems are transformed into a collage of tagged online images, a 3D shape, and even a set of interactive bar codes.

The results of the Poetry on the Road experiments can be seen online, along with interactive versions of the programs used to generate the images. The final body of work presents a highly diverse set of striking graphics that give insight into the wide range of ways in which code can be used to visualize words as graphics.

4.12 *Poetry on the Road*
Boris Müller
Sample covers from three editions of Poetry on the Road, designed by Boris Müller. The details show compositions created as visualizations of some of the individual pieces of poetry.

Keyboard user input

Each letter and character on a computer keyboard is assigned a numeric value, derived from its corresponding ASCII value. These values are used to allow word processing programs to differentiate between specific key presses. Programming languages can capture individual user keystrokes as they are typed, using them to create and define variables that define specific shape and graphical attributes (e.g., color, height, shape, or size). Lines of typed letters and words can therefore be visually abstracted into a series of colors, shapes, forms, and graphics that correspond to words typed into the keyboard. Dynamic visual patterns can be generated as a direct visual response to user keyboard input. A kind of "visual typewriter" can be created in which unique letter combinations, words, and sentence are visualized as a unique set of shape and color patterns. The rhythms and tones of words, lines, and sentences are transformed into visual patterns.

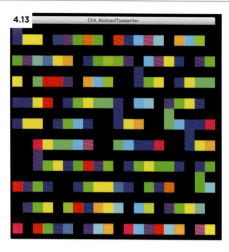

4.13 Keyboard generated shapes
Inspired by John Maeda's "Color Typewriter," this abstract composition of shapes and colors is generated by keyboard input. Typed letters are abstracted into colorful shapes that create a rhythmic composition of words and phrases.

Large text files

Just as single letters and short phrases can be drawn and re-visualized, so text sourced from large external data files can also be translated into visual information. Programming functions give designers the tools to read and analyze digital content from literally thousands of lines of text in the matter of a few seconds. Data values mined from a large piece of text can be abstracted into graphical visualizations or used to re-draw or alter the typographic style of the words themselves.

Digital files of entire books can be quickly and efficiently read into a drawing program, computationally analyzed, dissected, and split into useful groups of paragraphs, sentences, or words. The repetitive processing power of the computer allows a single function, used to find and visualize a single word, to be repeated and applied thousands of times—and to thousands of words. The details and structural complexities of entire passages or pages of books can be quickly picked out and re-formatted into new visual formats (for example, as data-informed drawings or pieces of typography). Hidden patterns, connections, and characteristics within the text can be discovered, revealed, and visualized.

For example, counting the number of times "key" words are repeated can reveal common ideas and themes within the text. The frequency of specific words can be found and saved as a number that is used to affect the visual style of the text—for example, to set the font size of the re-occurring words. This technique is commonly used in "Wordles," text clouds that highlight important phrases and word counts, but other visual formats can use it, as well.

FORM AND CONTENT

MOVEMENT AND INTERACTIVE TYPE

TEXT AS DATA SOURCE

EXTERNAL DATA

SPOTLIGHT ON ARIEL MALKA

CODE: COMPUTATIONAL TYPOGRAPHY

4.14

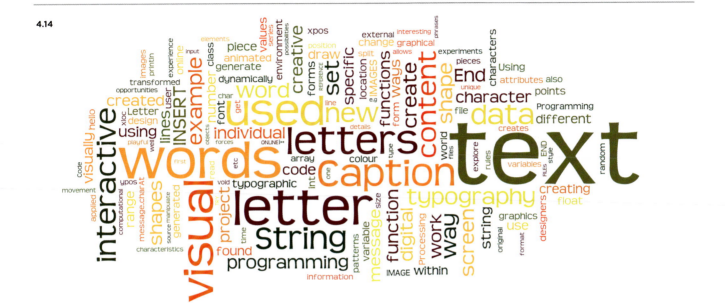

Digital text data is available from a number of different sources; for example, digital versions of many literary classics are freely available online to download from sites such as Project Gutenberg (www.gutenberg.org). A novel can be an interesting text data source; the ability to apply programming functions to an entire book creates fabulous opportunities for designers to manipulate the content, bring a fresh approach to a familiar text, and create design work that would be otherwise impossible to achieve. Entire passages and books of text can be re-rendered in a visual format that reflects the themes of their content. For example, the occurrences of specific words of phrases, or the rhythms and patterns within word groups, can be visually rendered and applied to the style of the typography, revealing patterns and characteristics of the text.

4.14 Wordle Cloud
A "Wordle" is an example of a "word cloud," which visualizes the relative frequency of words in a piece of text. This example shows the occurrences of words within this chapter. The Wordle visualizer is available at www.wordle.net.

EXEMPLAR

Stephan Thiel: Understanding Shakespeare

The Understanding Shakespeare project is a good example of data being used to visually inform the content of a piece of text, changing the way it is read and understood. The project, completed as a graduate project by then interface design student Stephan Thiel, explores and examines the works of Shakespeare. Thiel uses programming to extract and graphically represent specific pieces of information found within the text. By using code to re-visualize parts of Shakespeare's plays, the project reveals previously hidden elements of underlying narrative within the text and opens up new ways to read the work. The project uses programming tools to analyze the plays in five distinct ways, producing for each one a set of images that graphically summarize key elements found with each of the narratives, thus re-presenting this imposing body of work in a succinct and visually striking format.

Programming functions are used to select and show frequently used words for the characters in each play; sentences that summarize speeches; instances of statements beginning with personal pronouns, such as I, me, we, and so on; stage directions to indicate dramatic entrances and exits; and popular elements of each play, according to Google searches. The outcome in each case graphically presents an overview of the play. For each data search, a set of large-scale prints is produced, allowing viewers to get a broad visual overview of the patterns and rhythms within the dramatic structure of each play. All the information is summarized and re-presented in book format.

Understanding Shakespeare is a great example of visual storytelling in which programming methods have been creatively applied to the field of graphical communication. The designer has used and applied data in a thoughtful and meaningful way, applying the capability of code to extract specific words and phrases to create a visual, design-led outcome. The final results are a strong set of images that provide a fresh visual approach to an old and familiar text.

4.15 *Understanding Shakespeare* **Stephan Thiel** Example images from the project, which generated dynamic visualizations of some of Shakespeare's most famous works, allowing viewers to "read" and understand the familiar texts in a new way.

FORM AND
CONTENT

MOVEMENT
AND
INTERACTIVE
TYPE

**TEXT
AS DATA
SOURCE**

EXTERNAL
DATA

SPOTLIGHT ON
ARIEL MALKA

CODE:
COMPUTATIONAL
TYPOGRAPHY

EXTERNAL DATA

As well as using and revealing information and characteristics from within a piece of writing, the visual style of a piece of digital text can also be influenced by data sources external to the text. External information that has a direct relevance to or connection with the content of the text can be used to change the details of its shape and form, creating visual compositions that are visually and intellectually stimulating, presenting the words in a format that reveals new aspects and associations in the text that would otherwise be hidden. Interesting visual connections can be made that encourage viewers to read the text in a new way, establishing new connections that draw attention to the links between the text and its wider context or environment. For example, Twitter activity, GPS data, or other online activity, can be linked to passages of text to reveal the online activity surrounding specific text or to link the words to a specific location or landscape. Text can even be linked to sound files; code interprets elements of the audio track to generate a visual rhythm within the typography. Creating a link between data and typography makes a direct connection between the meaning and the visual attributes of words, which are defined by the data itself. Using and applying data to text and typography this way provides a designer with a host of new creative tools to communicate visually meaningful aspects of written content.

EXEMPLAR

4.16

4.16 *Generative Gatsby*
Vladimir V. Kuchinov
A visual re-working of the novel *The Great Gatsby* (1925) in which the rhythms and notes from jazz music scores have been used to re-interpret the typography of the original text.

FORM AND CONTENT

MOVEMENT AND INTERACTIVE TYPE

TEXT AS DATA SOURCE

EXTERNAL DATA

SPOTLIGHT ON ARIEL MALKA

CODE: COMPUTATIONAL TYPOGRAPHY

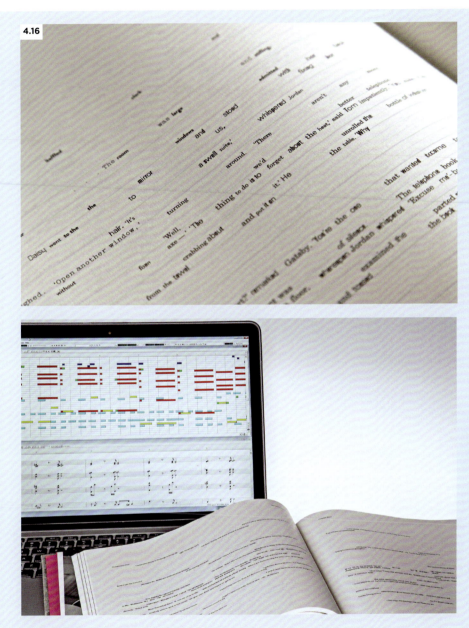

4.16

Vladimir V. Kuchinov: Generative Gatsby

Generative Gatsby is a project created by Vladimir V. Kuchinov in which F. Scott Fitzgerald's novel, *The Great Gatsby* (1925), has been re-imagined by altering the typography of the original prose using data from the rhythms of nine "big band" jazz standards from the 1920s. The musical scores, which could have played at Gatsby's parties, are used as templates for the code-based typography, in which each note's pitch, velocity, position, and duration are used to determine the positioning and style of the letters and words on the page. Furthermore, each instrument in the musical arrangement (piano, guitar, bass, brass, and percussion) is given a specific typeface considered to be evocative of the instrument's visual or emotional attributes. For example, the strings of the jazz guitar are represented by a modern thin typeface (Brandon Grotesque Thin) and drums and percussion are represented by a classic typewriter font (Remington Typewriter) evocative of the rhythmic, percussive sounds of typewriters in the 1920s. The final layouts produced by this generative design process highlight the rhythms of the jazz era, transforming the novel into a visual typographic expression of the musical styles of the Roaring Twenties.

SPOTLIGHT ON

Ariel Malka

Ariel Malka is a designer and programmer who has created a range of interactive projects. Most of his creative research is focused on experimenting with different forms of interactive typography. His work is characterized by the creation of environments that transform words into animated, fluid strings and ribbons of text, allowing the user to read and experience the content in a playful and engaging way. His research and experiments are well documented on his website (chronotext.org). Two typically interesting outcomes for his ongoing creative research process are "Javascriptorium" and a more recent interactive transformation of James Joyce's *Ulysses* (1922): "He Liked Thick Word Soup."

4.17

4.17 *Javascriptorium* **Ariel Malka**
Ariel Malka uses programming to generate dynamically animated and interactive versions of religious spiritual texts; these are beautifully poetic interactive typographic pieces that explore the relationship between text and content.

4.18

4.18 *He Liked Thick Word Soup* **Ariel Malka**
Ariel Malka's app turns sections of the text from James Joyce's *Ulysses* (1922) into interactive ribbons of text. The act of reading becomes an intricate, challenging, but pleasurable experience that resonates with the characteristics of the original work.

FORM AND CONTENT

MOVEMENT AND INTERACTIVE TYPE

TEXT AS DATA SOURCE

EXTERNAL DATA

SPOTLIGHT ON ARIEL MALKA

CODE: COMPUTATIONAL TYPOGRAPHY

4.18

How did you develop an interest in designing and programming?

A mix of passion and creative impulse, interleaved in a long trial-and-error process (I don't think I produced something worthwhile before the age of 30 . . .) It started by comics: reading them was not enough, I had to create my own. And then came video games . . . I received my first computer as a teenager in 1985 and it became obvious that I had to teach myself programming in order to create games.

Recipe: 1) Insert a Konami game cartridge into your MSX computer while turned-on. 2) If the hardware did not short-circuit, write a program in BASIC for "dumping" the memory on screen. 3) Decrypt the soup of hexadecimal numbers (which are bits of images or music? which are instructions for the Z80 processor? . . .)

Where do you look to find creative inspiration for your work: Who or what motivates and inspires you?

Inspiration is usually not the problem: opening a good book at a random page, stumbling upon a soundtrack on ubuweb, discovering stunning architecture on Flickr. The challenge is more to liberate enough time for digesting and processing all these inspirational gems (and then produce a new artwork, which is my primary motivation).

Why do you code? Do you think that there are specific qualities or characteristics of the programming world which open up creative possibilities?

Without the ability to code, your creativity may soon become limited by the metaphors imposed by "mainstream" authoring tools. Besides, producing a decent interactive application requires skills and talent in both programming and design (that being said, locking a software-engineer and an art-director in the same room for enough time is not necessarily the best option . . .) I believe that cultivating your own "hybrid" mind-set is the optimal creative strategy.

In what ways do you think that creating interactive type changes or enhances the reader's experience of the original text?

Instead of responding directly, I prefer creating an artwork asking similar questions and let the audience provide answers. For instance, my latest piece ("He Liked Thick Word Soup") is a mobile app for reading James Joyce's *Ulysses* with your fingers. Is it a new way to experience the original text? Probably, according to the feedback received so far. I invite everyone to judge by themselves.

Is it important that the text in your work is "readable" for the user?

Ideally, text in my work should be not only readable but also touchable, zoomable, copyable, utterable, linkable. It's probably going to take a while to develop and integrate all the required software components.

You have created a wide range of projects and design work; is there a particular piece or project of which you are most proud?

I'm particularly proud of the new-chronotext-toolkit (open-source on github), which I use for creating my own artworks and for making a living as a software architect the rest of the time. I shall be even prouder once the toolkit has evolved enough and other people start using it for creating their own text experiments!

Do you have any word of advice to young designers / students starting to explore this field of creative technology?

Take your time, build a self-confidence iteratively via micro successes, then allow yourself to get lost (and to reinvent the wheel . . .).

CODE: COMPUTATIONAL TYPOGRAPHY

Anatomy of Text as Data

Programming functions can be used to capture and display text on the screen. Text in a program is stored as String data. A String is a series of characters (usually letters) "strung together" between a set of speech marks:

```
// example String
String s = "a String of characters";
```

Individual letters or characters are stored as char data types.

```
char c = 'a'; // a single character
```

A String is essentially a list of individual characters and could be written as follows:

```
char[] letters = {'S', 't', 'r', 'i', 'n', 'g'};
```

String data can be displayed in many different ways and can be accessed from many different sources. Once saved or generated into the program, String data can be manipulated and re-formatted in a range of different visual ways.

Displaying and Formatting Text

Go to www.bloomsbury.com/richardson-data-driven, Chapter 4, and click on the project "Displaying Text."

Most programming languages have functions to display text on the screen. In Processing, the function to display words is the text() function. The text() function uses three parameters (arguments): a String of text to display, and a pair of numbers to determine the x and y location of the words on the screen.

```
text (String, x, y);
// put message on screen at x=10, y=50
text ("hello world", 10, 50);
```

In this example, a default font, size, and color are used. Additional functions can alter the size and color of the font. Font size can be set by the textSize() function. Font color is set using the fill() function:

```
textSize (48);
fill (255,0,0);
text ("hello", 10, 50);
```

Hello World

A Processing example of type drawn to the screen.

TIP: A list of other Processing functions used to set or control text on screen can be found online: https://processing.org/reference/text_.html

TRY IT

Use the text functions to write some text to the screen. Try different sizes, colors, and locations.

FORM AND
CONTENT

MOVEMENT
AND
INTERACTIVE
TYPE

TEXT
AS DATA
SOURCE

EXTERNAL
DATA

SPOTLIGHT ON
ARIEL MALKA

CODE:
COMPUTATIONAL
TYPOGRAPHY

Selecting and Controlling Fonts (PFont)

Go to www.bloomsbury.com/richardson-data-driven, Chapter 4, and click on the project "Using PFont."

In order to add and use a greater range of fonts in Processing, the PFont class is used. The PFont class can load fonts into a sketch, ready to display them on screen. Before a new font can be used, its font file has to be created and saved inside a "data" folder within the sketch; this is done via the Tools > Create Font menu, which creates the necessary font (.vlw) file.

Once the font file has been added into a data folder, it is ready to be loaded into the sketch via the PFont class. The loadFont() function loads the font file ready to use. The textFont() function selects the font to be used on screen.

```
PFont myFont; // create a new PFont object to use
// load the font, the file has to be in the data
folder
myFont = loadFont("LetterGothicStd-38.vlw");
// select the loaded font and set the size
textFont (myFont, 38);
text ("word", 10, 50);
```

Hello World

Hello World

Hello World

The Processing PFont class gives options for selecting and using a variety of fonts on the screen.

TRY IT

Create a font using the Processing menu.
Load and apply the font to alter the typographic style of the letters. Try different types of typography.

Using Variables with Text

Go to www.bloomsbury.com/richardson-data-driven, Chapter 4, and click on the project "Text and Variables."

Using variables instead of fixed values allows the text to change its position or content. The data elements used in the text() function to set the content and location of words can be replaced with more useful, variable values. A String variable can replace the first parameter and number variables can replace the values that set the text's x and y screen location:

```
String message = "hello world";
float xpos = 100;
float ypos = 50;
text (message, xpos, ypos);
```

A change to the content of any of the variables will change the way the text is displayed. Using variables can dynamically alter both the position and the content of the text on screen. In the following example, a variable is used to replace the fixed number that sets the x location. Changing the variable—for example, by increasing by 10—updates the x location of the text, making it scroll horizontally along the screen.

```
float xpos = 10;
void draw() {
    text ("hello", xpos, 100);
    xpos += 10;
}
```

The system variables mouseX, mouseY can also be used to dynamically move text with the location of the mouse cursor.

```
void draw() {
    text ("hello", mouseX, mouseY);
}
```

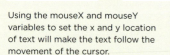

Using the mouseX and mouseY variables to set the x and y location of text will make the text follow the movement of the cursor.

TRY IT

Create some simple examples of words that move horizontally, move vertically, or follow the mouse.

As well as changing the location, variables can also dynamically change the content of text. In the following example, a String variable ("message") is used to set the words to be displayed. The content of the variable changes with the horizontal movement of the mouse. When the mouse is on the left side of the screen (<50) the value of the variable, "message," changes to "left," and when the mouse is on the right, the variable changes the text to "right."

```
String message ="";
void draw() {
    background(0);
    text (message, mouseX, 50);
    if (mouseX<50) message = "left";
    if (mouseX>50) message = "right";
}
```

Left   *Right*

Using a variable as the content of the text can create a simple type of interaction: The words can change as the mouse is moved to the left and right sides of the screen.

TRY IT

Create a variable to alter the content of the words on screen when the mouse is moved up and down.

Manipulating a String

Processing includes a range of functions useful for analyzing the characteristics of a String. Functions can be used to compare Strings, find specific characters, or switch between lower and uppercase. A sample of some of the main functions are listed:

charAt (n): finds the nth letter ("character") in a String.

indexOf(string): finds the first occurrence of specified String. Can be used for finding the first time a word or part of a word is used.

length(): gets the number of characters in piece a String.

equals(): compares one String to another.

subString(): finds a sub-section of a String.

split(): used to divide a String into separate sections.

Programming a computer to quickly sift through text in this way can be a useful source of creative and visual interpretation. A full reference list of String functions can be found at:

https://processing.org/reference/String.html

FORM AND
CONTENT

MOVEMENT
AND
INTERACTIVE
TYPE

TEXT
AS DATA
SOURCE

EXTERNAL
DATA

SPOTLIGHT ON
ARIEL MALKA

**CODE:
COMPUTATIONAL
TYPOGRAPHY**

Splitting Strings

Go to www.bloomsbury.com/richardson-data-driven, Chapter 4, and click on the project "Splitting Strings."

Moving and manipulating entire words as a single block has limited visual use. Manipulating the individual characters of a String can create more visually interesting results.

A String is a list, an array, of individual characters. Like any other array, a String has a "length()" function that returns the number of characters it contains:

```
String message = "hello world";
int numOfChars = message.length();
println (numOfChars); // outputs 11
```

A specific character within the String can be found using the charAt() function. The charAt() function returns the character found at a specific point (index) within a String. The first character is at index point 0 so is found by charAt(0);

```
String message = "hello world";
// finds the first character ('h')
message.charAt (0);
```

Every character in a String could be found and output as follows:

```
String message = "hello world";
println (message.charAt (0)); // prints 'h'
println (message.charAt (1)); // prints 'e'
println (message.charAt (6)); // prints 'w'
println (message.charAt (10)); // prints 'd'
```

A more efficient way of finding each character of a String in turn is to use a "for" loop, which provides a quick way of looping through the list of characters:

```
String message = "hello world";
for (int i=0; i<message.length(); i++) {
    char letter=message.charAt(i);
    println (letter);
}
```

By adding a text() function within the "for" loop, this basic structure can be used to place and draw each letter on the screen one at a time.

```
float xloc = 10; // starting loc for first letter
String message = "hello world";
for (int i=0; i<message.length(); i++) {
    char letter=message.charAt(i); // get a letter
    text (letter, xloc, 50); // draw a letter at an xloc
    xloc += 10 ; // increase xloc
}
```

NOTE: The variable "xloc" needs to be used to set the x position for each letter in turn so that they are all evenly spaced.

Splitting a String to draw letters one at time means that each character can be individually changed and drawn in a unique way. In the sample below, functions are added to the "for" loop to assign random size and color values to each character in a String.

```
float xloc = 10;
String message = "hello world";
for (int i=0; i<message.length(); i++) {
    char letter=message.charAt(i); // get a letter
    fill (random (255)); // select a random fill color
    // select a random text size
    textSize(random (4, 50));
    text (letter, xloc, 50);
    xloc += textWidth (letter);
}
```

random letters

Splitting a String of text into individual characters allows letters to be drawn individually, each at a different weight and height.

TIP: The textWidth() function is used to create an evenly spaced word; the width of the current each letter is found, and this value is used to re-calculate the position of the next letter.

Each individual letter is repeatedly re-drawn at a small random distance from its original location, creating a simple "animation" effect for each letter.

TRY IT

Create a sketch of randomly colored letters.
Use a draw() function to make the letters animate and move over time.

Adding Animation: Jiggle, Rotate

Go to www.bloomsbury.com/richardson-data-driven, Chapter 4, and click on the project "Animating Text."

Being able to find and draw each character in a String opens up opportunities to animate words by moving each letter independently. In the following example, a variable is used to randomly offset the "x" location of each letter and vary the overall appearance of the word. Putting the code to do this in a repeating "draw()" function continually re-draws the text and creates an overall "jiggle" effect of animated letters:

```
String message = "hello world";
void draw( ) {
    background (125);
    float xloc = 10;
    for (int i=0; i<message.length(); i++) {
        char letter=message.charAt(i);
        float offset_x = random (-3, 3);
        text (letter, xloc+offset_x, 50);
        xloc += textWidth (letter);
    }
}
```

TRY IT

Recreate the example.
Add a new variable to also offset the y position of the letters.

Letters as Dynamic Objects

Go to www.bloomsbury.com/richardson-data-driven, Chapter 4, and click on the project "Letter Class."

The ability to change and animate individual letters can be enhanced by using object oriented programming (OOP) techniques. Object oriented programming processes can enhance the behavioral, flexible qualities of individual letters, transforming each into an animated "reactive" object with its own set of functions, behaviors, and attributes.

OOP functions can be used to take individual letters and apply animated and interactive behaviors to each one. The following is sample "generic" Letter class that contains variables to store the letter, its location, and its speed. It also contains functions to move and draw the letter:

```
class Letter {
    float ypos;
    float xpos;
    char letter;
    float speed;
```

FORM AND CONTENT

MOVEMENT AND INTERACTIVE TYPE

TEXT AS DATA SOURCE

EXTERNAL DATA

SPOTLIGHT ON ARIEL MALKA

CODE: COMPUTATIONAL TYPOGRAPHY

```
Letter (char let, float x, float y) {
    letter = let;
    xpos = x;
    ypos = y;
    speed = random (1, 5);
}
void moveLetter() {
    ypos += speed;
}

void drawLetter() {
    text (letter, xpos, ypos);
}
}
```

Instances of this class are created using the "new" command, which calls the "constructor" function in the class:

```
Letter letter1 = new Letter ('a', 100, 200);
```

Once created, functions within the class to move and draw the letter instance are called as follows:

```
letter1.moveLetter();
letter1.drawLetter();
```

An array of Letter instances can be created from each individual character of a String. The following example takes a String and converts each character in turn into a new Letter instance:

```
String message = "drop";
Letter [] letters;
float xpos = 10;

void setup() {
    // create an array for the letters
    letters = new Letter [message.length()];
    for (int i=0; i<letters.length; i++) {
        // add an letter instance
        letters[i] = new Letter (message.charAt(i),
        xpos, 20);
        xpos += 10;
    }
}
```

Each instance of the letter object is created with a specific character, location, and random speed. The moveLetter() and drawLetter() functions can be called for each instance in the array to animate them.

```
void draw() {
    background (125);
    for (int i=0; i<letters.length; i++) {
        letters[i].moveLetter();
        letters[i].drawLetter();
    }
}
```

Using OOP in this way allows letters to become individually animated and reactive objects with the ability to move independently of one another. More functionality can be written into the Letter class to extend the range of movements and behaviors for each letter.

Processing: Using an object-oriented approach to drawing letters allows each letter to have its own set of behaviors.

TRY IT

Look at the online examples of the Letter class.
Try to create and apply your own Letter class.
Add a function to make each letter "bounce" off the edges of the screen.

Text as Data: Load Strings

Go to www.bloomsbury.com/richardson-data-driven, Chapter 4, and click on the project "Load Text as Data."

As well as using (short) String variables written inside the program, String data can be loaded in from an external source. The loadStrings() function imports the contents of an external text file and creates an array of its individual lines.

```
// create an array of the lines of text from an
external file
String [ ] lines = loadStrings ("wutheringHeights.
txt");
// display the number of lines in the text
println ("number of lines = " + lines.length);
```

NOTE: The text file to be loaded must be located in the Processing sketch's "data" folder. A resource of free downloadable books available as plain text (.txt) files can be found online at Project Gutenberg (www.gutenberg.org).

Once imported, every line of text in the array can be read and displayed on the screen:

```
float ypos = 20;
String [] lines = loadStrings ("wutheringHeights.
txt");
for (int i=0; i<lines.length; i++) {
  text (lines[i], 10, ypos); // draw a line of text
  // change the y position for the next line of text
  ypos += 10;
}
```

Using the split() or splitTokens() function, lines of text can be subdivided into arrays of individual words. Both the split() and the splitTokens() function "split" a String (e.g., a line of text) into an array of individual pieces (e.g., words). A specific character is used to determine where this split happens (commonly the space between each word). Unlike split(), splitTokens() can use more than one character to divide a String, and so can remove additional punctuation marks as well as spaces.

```
// example using split() and splitTokens()
String message = "Hi. A greeting!"; // String to be
divided up
// splits String at the spaces: creates an array of
3 words
String words1[] = split(message, " ");
// splits String at the spaces and removes the
punctuation (, and !)
String words2[] = splitTokens(message, " ,!");
```

Getting individual words from a large text file is a useful starting point for digging deeper into the text: for example, looking for patterns or word occurrences. The words in each line can be counted (to get an overall word count) or checked for number of occurrences of a specific word. In the following example, each line of text is split into words. Each word is then compared to see if it matches a character name from the novel. Each time a match is found, the "wordSearch" variable is increased by one.

```
String [ ] lines = loadStrings ("wutheringHeights.
txt");
int wordSearch=0;
int wordCount=0;
```

FORM AND
CONTENT

MOVEMENT
AND
INTERACTIVE
TYPE

TEXT
AS DATA
SOURCE

EXTERNAL
DATA

SPOTLIGHT ON
ARIEL MALKA

**CODE:
COMPUTATIONAL
TYPOGRAPHY**

```
for (int i=0; i<lines.length; i++) {
   String words [] = splitTokens (lines[i], "
,.;:!");
   wordCount += words.length;
   for (int n=0; n<words.length; n++){
      // look for a specific word
      if (words[n].equals("Heathcliff")) {
        wordSearch++;
      }
   }
}
// print the total number of words
println ("total words = " + wordCount);
// print the number of words matching the search
term
println ("word search count = " + wordSearch);
```

In this way, large amounts of text data can be easily sorted
and sifted, revealing hidden patterns of word usage that can
be visualized in a number of different ways.

CHAPTER FIVE
SEEING THE WORLD

"Vision is the art of seeing what is invisible to others."

Jonathan Swift

DIGITAL SPACES

Our modern environment has become a space increasingly filled with digital objects and experiences where the line between the physical and the virtual has blurred. Digital media is more flexible than ever; it is encountered in a huge variety of ways and places and surrounds us more and more in our daily lives. Technology has moved digital images from the constraints of a desktop computer screen to new environments and places, meaning that they can be encountered as a part of our everyday experience. Projected, interactive images are used to transform mundane, everyday spaces or objects (e.g., buildings, rooms, tables) into immersive and lively user environments. Large screen projections, small screen hand-held devices, and interactive surfaces use digital technology to augment retail spaces, galleries, museums, and other areas.

Retail spaces

Retail environments are focused on display and are always eager to use eye-catching ways of drawing attention to their brands and products. In the face of fierce competition from online shopping, brick-and-mortar stores have increasingly explored interactivity to inform, engage, and amuse, making shopping a more enticing experience. Bright digital displays are now a common feature of modern shopping; touch-screens offer information; monitors act as moving billboards. Images projected onto the wall or floor can be made interactive by the use of cameras and sensors that detect human movement and allow visitors to "kick" through virtual leaves or play and interact with virtual animals. In-store digital displays can include interactive virtual mirrors that allow shoppers to preview themselves wearing different outfits from the store.

Large storefronts and window displays can be transformed with cameras and sensors into interactive experiences that generate interactive graphics or messages by sensing and responding to human movement in front of the store.

Gallery/museum spaces

Set against an increasingly technological background and competing for the attention of an increasingly tech-savvy audience, museums and galleries have also become increasingly keen to make use of interactive technology to enhance the visitor experience and to increase engagement with and understanding of items in the museum collection.

Interactive devices allow the experience of an exhibition to extend beyond the traditional glass case and the "look-but-don't-touch" approach into immersive large- and small-screen environments that allow the visitor to explore items of a collection or navigate through an exhibition in more depth. This is an emerging area—a new way for museums to deliver content.

Touch screens and protected images create interactive information graphics: 3D models, interactive maps, and graphics can be useful visual ways of conveying detailed information that would be otherwise hard to explain. Smartphone technology allows visitors to find out more information about specific elements in an exhibition or help them navigate a path around a show. Augmented reality technology can also be used to expand the physical environment of an exhibition or museum, bringing to life places, people, environments, and situations that help to tell the story of a show. Viewers can discover background details or be lead on a journey through a historical account. Revealing the events, descriptions, and stories behind the objects on display helps to create an immersive experience that situates the visitor in a specific place or time relevant to the display—a type of time travel.

DIGITAL SPACES

LARGE SCREEN PROJECTIONS: BODY MOVEMENT

SMALL SCREEN DISPLAYS: DIGITAL MIRRORS

WAYS OF SEEING

SEEING PEOPLE

SEEING DISTANCE AND PROXIMITY

SPOTLIGHT ON WATSON AND GOBEILLE

CODE: SEEING THE WORLD

Game play

Being engaged with content does not have to be about filling a head with facts and figures; game play and lightheartedness in general can also be a good way to engage viewers and visitors. Less-tangible information can be offered to visitors in an exploratory way. Wrapping ideas and concepts into a game environment is a good way to allow people to discover and explore a subject—one that is especially useful for exploring more abstract ideas, such as co-operation or creativity.

Interactive environments that sense or detect human movement can immerse viewers in a powerful and engaging way, breaking the barrier of the screen, mouse, and keyboard, leading to a fulfilling interactive experience. Work that playfully engages viewers in an "all round" experience, in which body movement is used as trigger for interaction, can be a powerful way of involving audiences for both educational and commercial purposes.

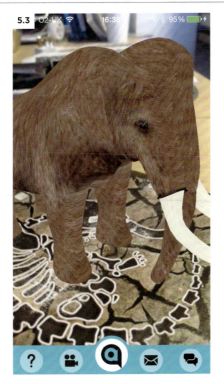

5.3 Large-scale Markers
This test for an augmented reality concept makes use of large-scale markers to produce very big AR experiences—in this instance, a virtual mammoth.

THE **WORLD**
ACCORDING TO
Beᴅe

5.2 Bede's World Museum
Augmented Reality (AR) is used as a way of bringing objects in a museum to life. When viewed through a smart phone or similar device, objects become "augmented" with additional, digitally created, images or 3D models. The Bede's World Museum app uses AR to bring viewers face to face with the ghost of the Venerable Bede.

LARGE SCREEN PROJECTIONS: BODY MOVEMENT

Large screen projections allow environments to respond to the presence of figures within a space; they can be used in many different contexts. Whether in a large shopping center window display or in the controlled interior space of a museum or gallery, a large digital projection can create playful immersive environments that the user can feel fully part of. These types of environments often track and use large user gestures and actions that involve the whole figure. They may use green screen technology in which people see themselves superimposed onto a new background and thus "transported" into a new world. Graphical objects and animations can interact with the gestures of the users, perhaps attracted to or repelled to the users' figures as they move, kick, or wave their arms. These types of interactive environments generate a range of different interactive responses. As well as being projected onto a wall or building, large scale interactives can be projected from above onto a floor, tracking the positions of people as they move through a space. Interactive graphics on a floor surface react to figures as they move in and across the floor (e.g., scattering leaves, etc.).

EXEMPLAR

Yoram Mesuere and Bagger: Vitrine

Vitrine is an experimental interactive window installation, created by the interactive design agency Baggar working alongside Yoram Mesuere. Graphical shapes initially collect and move together around the logo at the center of the screen. The movement of passers-by in front of the window display is monitored by cameras and used to trigger the shapes to animate and follow the viewers as they pass.

A computer set-up is used to track the general positions of people in front of the screen. This allows the graphics to move to the general location of the users, rather than have to track outlines or gestures exactly. The interaction creates a simple yet strong connection between the viewer and the image and gives immediate visual feedback, allowing the viewer to see the effects of their movements on the animations. The movements of the shapes have an organic feel; the shapes gradually flock and swarm together like birds or leaves blown by the wind. The naturalistic qualities of the movement add a sense of simple pleasure to the interactive experience that masks the digital and computational processes.

5.4 *Vitrine*
Baggar and Yoram Mesuere
An experimental interactive window installation, created by the design agency Baggar working alongside Yoram Mesuere.

DIGITAL SPACES

LARGE SCREEN PROJECTIONS: BODY MOVEMENT

SMALL SCREEN DISPLAYS: DIGITAL MIRRORS

WAYS OF SEEING

SEEING PEOPLE

SEEING DISTANCE AND PROXIMITY

SPOTLIGHT ON WATSON AND GOBEILLE

CODE: SEEING THE WORLD

SMALL SCREEN DISPLAYS: DIGITAL MIRRORS

5.5

Small display screens can employ cameras as image recognition devices, often to create single-user interactions in which a screen reacts to the viewer as a kind of digital mirror. A live feed can make real-time changes to the viewer's image, manipulating or digitally enhancing it. Graphics and images can also augment the image—for instance, gravitating toward the body or face.

The magic of a digital mirror can transform the images of the viewers as they peer into it. A kind of "Alice In Wonderland" effect occurs as the viewers see themselves in a new way, transformed by the technology. The viewers may see themselves wearing new digital clothing, masks, or head wear; their on-screen images may become a magnet for creatures to swarm towards or even begin to sprout new limbs or wings. Seeing your own image changed with even simple transformations can make for a fascinating experience.

5.5 *You Fade To Light*
Random International
A large-scale installation created using a grid of LEDs and a camera-based motion tracking system. Working as a kind of digital looking-glass grid, viewers are encouraged to engage physically to create images of themselves.

EXEMPLAR

Moving brands:
LC Fashion show

Commissioned by the London College
of Fashion, Moving Brands created a
reactive tabletop surface as a way of
interactively showcasing all 500 pieces
of work in the Graduate Portfolio
Exhibition.

Each student in the exhibition was
represented by a specially designed
postcard, which had a sample visual
of their printed work on the front,
and a unique identifying tag on the
back. When placed on the surface of
the table, the tag on each postcard
triggered a set of digital images
from the corresponding student's
portfolio. Moving the card created
the interaction; turning and rotating
the card allowed the viewer to shuffle
through the image set.

The project uses a combination
of Processing and Reactivision
technologies to create the printed tags
as interactive triggers. A webcam and
infrared lamp beneath the surface
of the table were used to track the
location of the tags on the table and
send the information to the computer,
which projected the digital images
from below.

The overall experience beautifully
combines the physical quality of the
postcard with the digital projection
on the table, making the interaction
intuitive and the experience
compelling: ordinary printed postcards
are transformed into something
interactive, surprising, even magical.

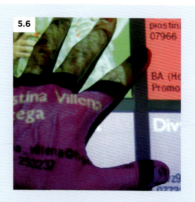

5.6

DIGITAL
SPACES

LARGE SCREEN
PROJECTIONS:
BODY
MOVEMENT

SMALL SCREEN
DISPLAYS:
DIGITAL MIRRORS

WAYS OF
SEEING

SEEING
PEOPLE

SEEING DISTANCE
AND PROXIMITY

SPOTLIGHT ON
WATSON AND
GOBEILLE

CODE:
SEEING THE
WORLD

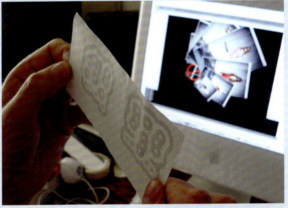

5.6 *Interactive Portfolio Table*
for the London College of
Fashion, Moving Brands
Screens can be turned into
responsive table surfaces that
react to objects placed on
them, as demonstrated in this
imaginative design solution
created by Moving Brands, to
showcase the work of over
500 final-year students' virtual
portfolios. Special "fiducial"
markers were used on cards as
triggers to project images for
each student. The combination
of the physical (printed
cards) with the digital creates
an engaging and intuitive
experience.

WAYS OF SEEING

There are lots of different ways in which the computer can "see" in order to detect the presence and the gestures of humans, objects, lights, and so on. As an input device, the computer is usually used as a "blind" observer on the world, limited to sensing movement via only mouse and keyboard input. As a sensing device, however, the computer is much more sophisticated than that, and capable of responding to a wide range of input types. Many artists, designers, and creative technologists have realized that limiting the scope of computer input and interaction to keyboard and mouse input ignores the immense capability of the computer as a sophisticated input and data processing device. In recent years, therefore, artists, designers and programmers have worked hard to enthusiastically explore the capabilities of the computer as a multi-sensory device, creating digital environments that can sense the world around them.

The main area of activity in this area has centered on the computer as a seeing device ("computer vision"). Allowing the computer to access and process visual information has proved to be of particular interest to creative artists and designers. Recent advancements in computer processing have made computer vision a field that has been applied to a range of creative projects. Despite the increased sophistication of technology, the same basic concepts are still used. With the right tools and resources (and there are lots online), a programmer can allow a computer to see objects and people quickly and with little expense.

Computer "vision"

The most common way of connecting a computer to its outside environment is by attaching it to a camera—for example, a webcam—which becomes the "eye" of the device. Once connected to a camera, the computer acts as the "brain," processing and interpreting visual information in order to make sense of the world. There are a few different approaches and techniques that can be used to detect different types of object and movement.

Seeing Color

One of the main ways in which the computer can make sense of the world around it is by looking at color information through the lens of a camera. A moving image from a camera feeds sequences of images to a computer at a rate of about 28 frames per second. Each individual frame from the video source contains hundreds of individual boxes (pixels), which are captured and processed by the computer as a list of color values. For example, a camera that captures footage at an image size of 320 x 240 pixels creates a series of individual frames, each of which contain 76,800 individual pixels of color. Code can be used to sort through each of the thousands of color values, looking for specific shades or hues, and it can use this information to help the computer to find patterns, identify shapes, and make sense of the visual world around it. Using code to sort, select, and manipulate the color data from pixel information is therefore a key part of computer vision.

See Code section: Color as a Data Type (page 152).

EXEMPLAR

Matthieu Savery: Pixel Data

Pixel Data is a free app, created by Matthieu Savary, that re-examines the visual possibilities of smartphone photography. The app treats photographic images as sets of color information and uses the data to re-arrange the pixels of an image using parameters such as tone and color value. After being broken into its individual bits of color information, each image is re-organized according to different parameters, such as tone or RGB values. The parameters by which the pixels are re-organized are adjustable via a series of on-screen sliders.

By sorting color data according to logical values, the app challenges the assumption that the pixels in a digital photograph have to be viewed in a "correct" order, and allows users to re-interpret their photography to create abstract and impressionistic images. The resultant confetti-like images present a fresh way of thinking about the way in which the color information of a smartphone image is processed and displayed.

DIGITAL SPACES

LARGE SCREEN PROJECTIONS: BODY MOVEMENT

SMALL SCREEN DISPLAYS: DIGITAL MIRRORS

WAYS OF SEEING

SEEING PEOPLE

SEEING DISTANCE AND PROXIMITY

SPOTLIGHT ON WATSON AND GOBEILLE

CODE: SEEING THE WORLD

5.7 *Pixel is Data*
Matthieu Savary
Sample images from the app that computationally re-organizes pixel data from smartphone photographs. Changing the settings produces different sets of digitally "impressionistic" results.

Static Images

Every digital bitmap image (gif or jpeg) is a collection of hundreds or thousands of individual color values: pixels. Even the most complex of digital images is actually a list, a mosaic, of individual squares of color. When using digital graphics software to select and apply a filter to an image (e.g., apply blur or contrast), the designer is actually getting the software to computationally manipulate and change the pixel information in the original image. Code, however, gives designers and programmers direct access to the list of individual color values in an image, allowing them to manipulate the color data in a more direct, "hands-on" way. This "direct access" to color data allows programmers to use code to extract and analyze the color data of a bitmap image in real time, as part of an interaction. This can be especially effective when applied to a sequence of moving images taken from a video feed.

See Code section: Get Color from a Static Image (page 152).

Moving Images

Lists of pixel color data from a live video source can be captured, searched through, and analyzed. Searching through and extracting individual color values from a live camera feed gives the designer a valuable way of observing the surrounding environment. Code can be used to search for and find sections of a video feed that contain a specific color (e.g., green) or find areas of extreme contrast, brightness, or darkness. Having the ability to find pre-defined colors or areas of particular brightness or darkness allows designers the

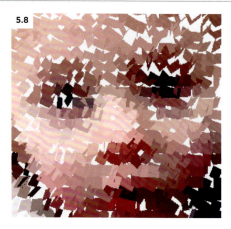

5.8

5.8 "Image mosaic" example
The color data from pixels in video images can be used to create "digital mirrors" in which the images are transformed into a moving mosaic of graphical shapes.

starting point to create environments that identify moving figures as colors, separate foreground and background elements, or track color or lights.

See Code section: Import a Live Video Source (page 155).

Techniques for finding color information can be applied in the creation of a number of types of interactive environment. Green screen techniques, which separate the background from foreground figures, can be used to replace the background of a scene with entirely new imagery or manipulate the visual effects on people in front of the camera. Similarly, finding very bright pixels can be used as a way of generating physical interactions based on the movement of LED lights or flashlights as they are waved in front of a screen, a way of interacting that is the basis behind the concept and technology of the Nintendo Wii.

See Code sections: Follow the Brightest Pixel (page 157) & Green Screening (page 158).

Green Screen Effects

• "Green screen" effects can be created by finding large areas of pixels of a specific single hue that form a background wall; these can be ignored or replaced, leaving the figure in the foreground.

• Areas of low brightness values can reveal the presence and movement of people; the shadows or silhouettes of figures can be found as they pass in front of or behind a screen.

• Finding and following the very brightest pixels in front of a camera is a simple way of tracking the movements of lights.

• An alternative to green screening is the "difference technique," which is a variation of the green screen concept. Color values of the empty environment are continually compared with color values of the current scene. Differences between the two indicate the presence of people entering the space.

DIGITAL
SPACES

LARGE SCREEN
PROJECTIONS:
BODY
MOVEMENT

SMALL SCREEN
DISPLAYS:
DIGITAL MIRRORS

**WAYS OF
SEEING**

SEEING
PEOPLE

SEEING DISTANCE
AND PROXIMITY

SPOTLIGHT ON
WATSON AND
GOBEILLE

CODE:
SEEING THE
WORLD

EXEMPLAR

5.9 *Party Wall* **Sennep**
Images of the interactive
projection created as part of
a wedding party. Dance-floor
movement is captured and used
to project images on to the wall.

Sennep: Party Wall

Party Wall was a specially
commissioned interactive projection
installation created for a post-
wedding celebration. The movement
of guests on the party dance floor is
tracked, and the amount of energy
is used to trigger a wall projection.
Little or no movement results in a
blank screen; however, as soon as
a certain level of physical energy is
detected by the system, large images
of the dancers are projected onto the
wall in a pixelated grid of dots. The
system, which responds to energetic
dance moves, therefore encourages
even greater participation from the
guests.

SEEING PEOPLE

Looking for color information is the simplest and quickest way of finding movement and the presence of figures within an environment. The techniques involved are useful for spotting something new or different in a space. Color information, however, cannot give any detailed information about the specific figures within the space—for example, the number of people or the locations of their faces, gestures, or limbs. This kind of detailed information requires more sophisticated methods of image processing and computer vision. These methods involve many more complex mathematical processes. Fortunately for creative designers, there are several libraries and resources available that can assist and make the process less painful. This is a summary of the main concepts.

Blobs

Being able to find shapes within an image is a sophisticated and powerful way of detecting the presence and movement people in a scene, and gives much more detail than simply comparing color values. The detection of shapes and figures is a part of computer vision called "Blob Detection," and it is very useful for finding outlines of people. Blob detection is complex mathematical way of finding similar areas within an image whose color and brightness stand out against the rest of the image. Finding shapes that contain areas of broadly similar colors and shades gives a much more detailed and useful picture regarding the numbers and the movements of people within a scene. Because blobs join broadly similar areas of color (e.g., skin tone and clothing colors) they therefore allow much greater accuracy in detecting the outlines of people and can also, importantly, track and follow individual figures as they move across a scene. Blobs not only accurately detect shapes, but they can also distinguish among and follow different individuals. Both of these capabilities are useful for generating user interaction.

Finding edges

Blob detection of people in a scene can be used to find the edges of figures in an environment, which can be used as the basis of imaginative interactions that work with and around the participants' body shapes. Animated lines or graphics can be attracted to the outline of person's body; digital "rain" can settle onto hands or arms; graphics can grow and emerge from around the body outline. Locating the shapes and outlines of people in this way helps to effectively place them in the center of an interactive screen or game, giving a fuller illusion of interaction and adding to the level of engagement, enjoyment, and "magic."

Computer Vision Libraries for Processing

The Processing environment includes a range of extra libraries that are used to extend the capability of the programming language in specific ways. Amongst these are libraries specifically built to enable Processing to engage in computer vision: seeing and analyzing the presence of people within a live video image. Two good examples of these include BlobDetection (http://www.v3ga. net/processing/BlobDetection/) and OpenCV for Processing (https://github.com/atduskgreg/ opencv-processing). A full list of the libraries, including ones used for "computer vision," can be found online at: https://processing.org/ reference/libraries/

DIGITAL
SPACES

LARGE SCREEN
PROJECTIONS:
BODY
MOVEMENT

SMALL SCREEN
DISPLAYS:
DIGITAL MIRRORS

WAYS OF
SEEING

SEEING
PEOPLE

SEEING DISTANCE
AND PROXIMITY

SPOTLIGHT ON
WATSON AND
GOBEILLE

CODE:
SEEING THE
WORLD

EXEMPLAR

5.10 *The Treachery of Sanctuary*
Chris Milk
Images from the interactive triptych in which participants use their bodies to create hybrids of human and bird-like creatures. The direct physicality of the interaction creates a remarkable transformation of the human form.

Chris Milk:
The Treachery of Sanctuary

The Treachery of Sanctuary is a large-scale interactive installation, consisting of three projected panels. Each panel uses a projected silhouette of the participant's body, interactively manipulating it with images of birds to represent the narrative of birth, death, and transfiguration. As users in front of the screen move, their projected body shape is digitally transformed into a flock of flying birds ("birth"), into a figure attacked by birds ("death"), or into a figure sprouting wings ("transfiguration"). The visual transformation of the user's body shape creates a strong emotional link with the theme. The simplicity of the interaction, together with black and white color scheme, adds beauty and elegance to the overall effect.

The shadows and movements of the user in front of each panel are captured using a Kinect camera. The code, written as an openFrameworks application, processes the information from the Kinect and connects to the graphics software, created in Unity, which created the animated, interactive birds.

Finding individuals

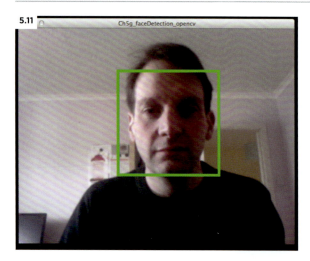

5.11

5.11 The ability to track faces is useful starting point for creating interactions based around individual users.

The ability of blobs to track and locate faces and individuals in a scene gives creative designers greater scope to develop group-based interactions, which include and involve the participation of several people at once. Animations, graphics, games, and interactions can be individually focused to follow single players within a group, while new users can be detected, triggering their own new sets of animated images and graphics. Virtual clothing or costumes can move with each user; individual styles of animation and graphics can be introduced for each new player in the scene.

Finding Faces

In addition to locating edges and tracking individuals in a scene, blob detection processes can also find and recognize faces. This is useful for graphics and animations that work by locating the head and face portions of a figure. Virtual disguises—hats, ears, masks—can appear on and around the faces of each user, animating and changing with each individual.

EXEMPLAR

Hellicar and Lewis: Interactive mask

Hellicar and Lewis are a creative team who blend technology, art, and design to create a range of interactive experiences for a wider range of clients and contexts, including fashion, performance, art, and education. Their work uses interaction to explore the relationships between viewers, spaces, and technology and brings together influences from several different art and science disciplines.

5.12 *Diaghilev Mask*
Hellicar and Lewis
Face-tracking software is used to find users in the scene and position the graphical animal masks onto the faces of the participants.

DIGITAL
SPACES

LARGE SCREEN
PROJECTIONS:
BODY
MOVEMENT

SMALL SCREEN
DISPLAYS:
DIGITAL MIRRORS

WAYS OF
SEEING

**SEEING
PEOPLE**

SEEING DISTANCE
AND PROXIMITY

SPOTLIGHT ON
WATSON AND
GOBEILLE

CODE:
SEEING THE
WORLD

5.12

Hellicar and Lewis: Diaghilev mask

The interactive mask project was commissioned by the Victoria and Albert Museum, London, in collaboration with their educational department to coincide with their Diaghilev exhibition. Picking up on the theme of theatrical masks, the interactive exhibit uses face recognition code to apply digital masks to participants in front of a computer camera. Specially written programming code creates each mask design and tracks the movement of the user wearing it.

Other pieces of interactive installation created by Hellicar and Lewis include Uniqlo Stripes, a commissioned wallbased interactive installation with the theme of stripes developed to help promote an event for the fashion label Uniqlo, and Norwegian Wood, an audioresponsive projection for the premiere of the film adaptation of the book Norwegian Wood, by Haruki Murakami, in London at the Haunch of Venison Gallery, which references elements of the film and traditional imagery of Japanese seasons.

SEEING DISTANCE AND PROXIMITY

Regular digital cameras, or webcams, can be used very effectively in computer vision projects to detect colors or shapes; however, they are limited in their capability to detect depth or specific user movements. The Kinect is a more sophisticated camera set-up that can detect both.

The gaming industry has, over recent years, been at the forefront in the development of new technology of computer vision in order to find new, immersive new ways for gamers to play and interact with gaming consoles. For example, Nintendo's innovative hand-held Wii motion and gesture sensors opened up new ways of thinking about traditional game controllers.

Each development of innovative commercial devices and technology is quickly seized upon by creative developers keen to explore wider creative uses and applications for the technology. One recent example is the Kinect, launched by Xbox, a powerful device that can detect a range of human movements and gestures. The device itself contains a "regular" RGB camera, plus an infrared camera and infrared light (used to detect depth and gesture). Although usually used with Xbox, the Kinect can be used as a stand-alone camera connected directly to a computer and used as a sophisticated sensor for developing interactive applications.

Several code libraries have been developed that allow direct access to the sensory information of the Kinect, allowing programmers access to a scene as a conventional (RGB) image, detect distance, and sense full-body physical gestures.

5.13

5.13 The Kinect camera has a built-in RGB camera, infrared light, and depth sensor, which can be used to visualize body movement, gesture, and proximity to the camera.

5.14

Depth camera

In addition to the regular camera view of a scene, the Kinect's camera device is also able to create a "depth image" of an environment: a grayscale image in which the color value of each pixel accurately relates to its distance from the camera. Objects that are closest to the camera appear as white, and those furthest away as black. The result is a "depth image." Differentiation between the proximity of objects from the camera means that objects in the foreground can be more easily tracked while background elements can be ignored or removed.

5.14 An example of a regular (RGB) image (right) and a "depth" image (left) captured by the Kinect camera connected to a computer device. Dan Shiffman's Processing library, "Open Kinect for Processing," is used to extract the depth image. Details available at: http://shiffman.net/p5/kinect/

Open Kinect for Processing
Processing includes some code libraries that enable the code to connect to and use the Kinect camera and its depth information. A good resource is Daniel Shiffman's Open Kinect for Processing (http://shiffman.net/p5/kinect/), which provides a useful starting point for connecting to and using the Kinect as an image data source.

DIGITAL SPACES

LARGE SCREEN PROJECTIONS: BODY MOVEMENT

SMALL SCREEN DISPLAYS: DIGITAL MIRRORS

WAYS OF SEEING

SEEING PEOPLE

SEEING DISTANCE AND PROXIMITY

SPOTLIGHT ON WATSON AND GOBEILLE

CODE: SEEING THE WORLD

EXEMPLAR

5.15

5.15 *Body Dysmorphia*
Robert Hodgin
The Kinect sensor creates a 3D "map" of a figure that can be computationally adjusted to create real-time distortions of the viewer's image.

Robert Hodgin: Body Dysmorphia

Body Dysmorphia uses a Kinect sensor to create a real-time interactive visualization of body dysmorphia disorder, a condition in which the sufferer is excessively concerned about a perceived physical defect. Proximity data from the Kinect camera is used to get visual information about the viewer, which is computationally adjusted and re-drawn to create a live distorted mirror. Surface information obtained from the camera is pushed out or in to make the subject fatter or thinner, morphing the viewer's real-time form into one that is either excessively bloated or emaciated.

Gesture detection

As well as being able to sense distance and depth, the Kinect camera can detect individual figures, find and track hand positions, and even recognize hand gestures and full body movements. The ability to accurately track hand and body movement creates a foundation for fully immersive interactive experiences in which the user's body becomes the game controller, intuitively involved in the environment. It is a powerful feature that has been explored and exploited by several games and interactive environments.

Hand tracking allows users to playfully engage with gesture-based screens or interactive table surfaces. Full-body figure detection can be used to create immersive large screen experiences, which playfully engage single or multiple users.

5.15

Infrared and Visual Noise

An infrared light source and camera are very useful for detecting shapes or figures in a scene. Infrared lights are often used in security camera devices; they emit a strong light source that humans cannot see but that infrared cameras can. Infrared lights can be purchased from security suppliers. Webcams cannot usually see infrared light because they have a special filter that blocks it out, but a programmer can "hack" one to make it an infrared camera by finding and removing the filter.

One problem with using a normal camera for figure detection is other light sources, especially projectors or display screens, add extra light that interferes—lots of "visual noise" that makes the job of figure detection much more difficult for the camera. Throwing an infrared spotlight over a scene and using a camera that only sees areas lit up with the infrared is a way of removing all the visible light sources that cause interference, allowing the camera to detect the people in the space.

EXEMPLAR

5.16

5.16

5.16 *Collections Wall*
Cleveland Museum of Art
An interactive wall featuring over 4,100 works of art from the permanent collection housed in The Cleveland Museum of Art. Touch-screen technology allows visitors to explore the collection and connect with objects, making their visit a more personal experience.

Local projects: Cleveland Museum of Art

Local Projects is a media design company that creates interactive experiences for public and museum spaces. With a focus on using technology to share stories, the company encourages new ways for people to interact with art, cities, and each other. In a recent major commission, Local Projects created an entire suite of interactive experiences for the Cleveland Museum of Art (Gallery One) aimed at inspiring visitors to explore and look again at the museum's collection in new and different ways.

Included among the outcomes was a set of carefully engineered individual "interactive lenses" placed throughout the exhibition space to allow visitors to enhance their experiences of the collection.

The Strike a Pose ("Sculpture lens") and Making Faces lenses are interactive encounters that use gesture and face recognition technology to encourage visitors to actively connect with the collection by seeing themselves in the art on display, encouraging visitors to think about how human form inspires art.

Strike A Pose is a game in which visitors to the museum imitate the unique pose of a sculpture from the collection. The interaction uses a Kinect to track the user's position and compare the key points against that of the sculpture. The code then rates the user's accuracy as

a score. Encouraging viewers to mimic the shape and position of a sculpture helps viewers to consider the artwork more closely and develop a physical connection with it.

The Make a Face interaction matches the user's facial expression to one of the artworks within the museum collection. The visitor's facial expression is captured via a webcam and its key features (distance between eyes, shape of mouth, etc.) are compared to a database of 180 artwork images to find a best match. A photo-strip of the matched faces can be emailed, shared, or displayed on a screen elsewhere in the museum.

5.17 *Make a Face*
Cleveland Museum of Art
by Local Projects
Face-recognition software
is used to match the facial
expression of the user with one
of the pieces of artwork in the
museum, creating a unique way
of exploring the collection.

DIGITAL
SPACES

LARGE SCREEN
PROJECTIONS:
BODY
MOVEMENT

SMALL SCREEN
DISPLAYS:
DIGITAL MIRRORS

WAYS OF
SEEING

SEEING
PEOPLE

**SEEING DISTANCE
AND PROXIMITY**

SPOTLIGHT ON
WATSON AND
GOBEILLE

CODE:
SEEING THE
WORLD

5.18

5.18 *Line and Shape*
**Cleveland Museum of Art by
Local Projects**
In this interactive, visitors draw
a line across the screen, which
is then matched with one of
the objects in the museum's
collection that contains a
similar line, allowing the visitor
to make new visual connections
between objects.

SPOTLIGHT ON

Theo Watson and Emily Gobeille

Theo Watson and Emily Gobeille
have produced a number of engaging
environments in which users playfully
explore and interact with animated
environments. Real-time green
screening of live images combine with
movement and gesture recognition to
create imaginary worlds in which the
participant can trigger rainstorms,
release lightning bolts, or produce
showers of leaves through movement
and gesture. The scale and elegance
of these creations, together with the
combination of creative technology
and reactive graphics, makes each
environment a charming experience.

Knee Deep

Knee Deep is an immersive installation
that uses computer technology and
real-time green screening effects
to encourage children to jump into
and explore new imaginary worlds
with their feet. A video feed of the
participants in front of the green
screen is fed into a computer and
processed (using openFrameworks) in
order to superimpose the background
and project the child into a fantasy
landscape. A computer vision system
tracks the positions and movements
of the children and generates the
dynamic animations. The overall effect
immerses the children in an exploratory
world in which they appear as giants,
controlling and commanding creatures
and environments that respond to their
activity.

5.19

DIGITAL SPACES

LARGE SCREEN PROJECTIONS: BODY MOVEMENT

SMALL SCREEN DISPLAYS: DIGITAL MIRRORS

WAYS OF SEEING

SEEING PEOPLE

SEEING DISTANCE AND PROXIMITY

SPOTLIGHT ON WATSON AND GOBEILLE

CODE: SEEING THE WORLD

5.19 *Knee Deep* Theo Watson and Emily Gobeille
Examples taken from the immersive interactive installation. Users are green-screened into one of several imaginary worlds and become active participants, interacting with characters and creatures by moving and stamping their feet.

CODE: SEEING THE WORLD

Color as a Data Type

Go to www.bloomsbury.com/richardson-data-driven, Chapter 5, and click on the project "Color as Data."

Creating a computer program that can "see" begins by getting and processing color information from a digital image; this can be from a single bitmap or even from a live video feed.

Color, like many other things in the computational environment, is defined and understood as a type of data. In Processing, the "color" data type is used to store and save color values that the code can refer back to later.

The following example creates two color data types of red and blue.

```
color c1 = color (255, 0, 0);
color c2 = color (0, 0, 255);
fill (c1);
stroke (c2);
```

Get Color from a Static Image

Go to www.bloomsbury.com/richardson-data-driven, Chapter 5, and click on the project "Color from Image."

Bitmap images are essentially a large list of individual (RGB) color values, drawn on the stage as individual pixels. Finding and using these values is the starting point to being able to create a program that can "see" and respond to the outside world.

Color information can be retrieved from either static or moving images. It is good to begin by looking at single static images. In Processing, images are loaded into the program by using the PImage class and the loadImage() function as follows:

```
PImage img;
img = loadImage ("face.jpg");
```

The image() function is used to place a loaded image onto the screen:

```
// draw the image on the screen
image (img, 100, 100);
```

TIP: In order to be loaded, the source image file has to be located in the "data" folder of the sketch.

Extracting color data of a SINGLE pixel in an image can be done by using the get() function, which gets color information from a specific x, y co-ordinate:

```
get (x, y);
// gets the color of a pixel x100, y10 from the image
"img"
img.get (100, 10);
```

Alternatively, color data can be extracted by referencing a specific pixel from the array list. (This is computationally a faster way.)

```
pixels[pixel_in_list];
// get the pixel at position 144 in the array
img.pixels[144];
```

These functions can be applied to get the color of a single pixel from a loaded image:

DIGITAL
SPACES

LARGE SCREEN
PROJECTIONS:
BODY
MOVEMENT

SMALL SCREEN
DISPLAYS:
DIGITAL MIRRORS

WAYS OF
SEEING

SEEING
PEOPLE

SEEING DISTANCE
AND PROXIMITY

SPOTLIGHT ON
WATSON AND
GOBEILLE

**CODE:
SEEING THE
WORLD**

```
size (800, 800);
PImage img = loadImage ("face.jpg"); // load image
image (img, 0, 0); // put image on stage

// save pixel color from image
color c1 = img.get(100, 100);
color c2 = img.pixels[400];

fill (c1); // use pixel color as fill color
rect (600, 0, 100, 100);
fill (c2);
rect (600, 150, 100, 100);
```

```
PImage img = loadImage ("me.jpg"); // load image
noStroke();
for (int y=0; y<img.height; y++) {
  for (int x=0; x<img.width; x++) {
    // find the color of the current pixel
    color c = img.get(x, y);
    fill (c); // use found color as the fill color
    ellipse (x, y, 1, 1); // redraw as a circle
  }
}
```

This is a simple type of "image manipulation" in which the color from a pixel in an image can be re-drawn as a shape, creating a mosaic effect.

An example of getting and displaying a color from a pixel in an image. A single pixel color from a photograph can be found and used as a fill color for other graphics on the screen.

TRY IT

Load an image into a Processing sketch.
Create the code to find and save a color value from a pixel in an image.
Use mouseX, mouseY to find pixel color of the mouse location as it moves over the image.

Get All Color Values from a Static Image

Go to www.bloomsbury.com/richardson-data-driven, Chapter 5, and click on the project "All Color from Image."

As well as getting a single value from an image, code can retrieve every color pixel from an image and re-draw them on the screen.

A nested "for" loop, one "for" loop inside the other, is a common way of sequentially going through each row and column of an image. The outer loop runs through the "y location" of each pixel; the inner loop gets the "x location" of each pixel. Using this structure and the get() function, the color of every pixel can be sequentially found and redrawn.

A pixelated "mosaic" image effect is achieved by re-drawing all the pixels. Color information from each pixel is found and used to draw each square..

TRY IT

Re-create the example above.
Alter the ellipse() function to re-draw each shape at a larger size.
Add spacing between each shape to alter the mosaic-like effect.

153

Extract More Color Information

Go to www.bloomsbury.com/richardson-data-driven, Chapter 5, and click on the project "Extract Color Data."

Additional functions can be used to extract more detailed color information from a pixel—for example, finding its brightness value or amounts of red, green, or blue.

The brightness() function finds the level of brightness in a color, saved as a value between 0 and 255, where 0 the darkest and 255 is the brightest.

```
color c1 = (64, 0, 0);
// finds the brightness level from a color
float br = brightness (c1);
```

The red(), green(), and blue() functions extract a value that gives the amount of each in a color:

```
// extracts the amount of red from a color
float r = red (c1);
float g = green (c1); // extracts the amount of green
float b = blue (c1); // extracts the amount of blue
```

This type of color information can be used to affect the way in which an image is re-drawn. For example, getting the brightness value of each pixel in the example code above can determine whether or not an individual "pixel" shape is drawn on the stage, so that only the darkest pixels are drawn.

```
// Use the following code within the example for loop
on page 153.
color c = img.get(x, y);
fill (c);
// get the brightness of the color
float br = brightness (c);
// only draw shape if brightness is less than 125
if (br<125) {
  ellipse (x, y, 1, 1);
}
```

Similarly, the brightness value of a color can be used to define the size of each circle shape, meaning that dark pixels are redrawn at the largest size. An example portion of the script is shown below:

```
color c = img.get(x, y);
fill (c);
// get the brightness
float br = brightness (c);
// map the brightness number to a useful range
br = map (br, 255, 0, 0, 20);
// use the brightness value to define the width and
height of the circle
ellipse (x, y, br, br);
```

A simple image-manipulation example in which the brightness of each pixel color is used to define the size of each square when it is re-drawn. Darker areas are drawn at larger sizes, creating an "impressionistic" style of image.

TIP: The map() function is used to translate the brightness levels (0 to 255) to a more useful number range (0 to 20).

TRY IT

Modify the original "pixel mosaic" example.
Add a function that finds the brightness of each color pixel.
Use the brightness value to only draw light/dark pixels.
Use the brightness value to modify the size of each pixel shape.

DIGITAL SPACES

LARGE SCREEN PROJECTIONS: BODY MOVEMENT

SMALL SCREEN DISPLAYS: DIGITAL MIRRORS

WAYS OF SEEING

SEEING PEOPLE

SEEING DISTANCE AND PROXIMITY

SPOTLIGHT ON WATSON AND GOBEILLE

CODE: SEEING THE WORLD

Import a Live Video Source

Go to www.bloomsbury.com/richardson-data-driven, Chapter 5, and click on the project "Input Video."

The examples have so far dealt with finding and using color information sourced from a static image file; however, these techniques can be equally applied to moving images sourced from a live video feed (from a webcam, for example). Switching the input source from a single image file to a live camera feed means that the same effects of extracting and manipulating color pixel information can be used to create a more visually dynamic effect.

TIP: In Processing, a "Video" library is used to play and display video files and to capture a live video feed from a camera.
A code "library" is a type of "add on," a way of extending the capability of a programming language.

Details are at: https://www.processing.org/reference/libraries/video/index.html

To begin, the Video library is imported into the Processing sketch:

```
import processing.video.*;
```

Once imported, the library can then be used to get and display a live video feed from any connected webcam or internal camera. A new Capture object is created that establishes a connection to a camera, begins the feed, and draws the image on the screen:

```
// CAPTURE AND DISPLAY A VIDEO FEED //
import processing.video.*;
Capture camera;
void setup() {
  size(800, 600);
  camera = new Capture(this, 320, 240);
  camera.start();
}

void draw() {
  if (camera.available()) {
    camera.read();
  }
  image(camera, 0, 0);
}
```

NOTE: The image capture for moving images is done within the looped draw() section of the program to ensure the image information is continually updated.

TRY IT

Create your own example that gets and views a live video input.

Once a live feed has been established, color information from each frame of the video can be extracted, using the same basic nested "for" loop structure that has been previously applied to the single static images. The result is a kind of digital mosaic, a type of pixelated mirror.

```
// PIXEL MIRROR FROM CAMERA FEED /////
import processing.video.*;
Capture camera;
float spacing = 5;
float dotSize = 4;
void setup() {
    size(800, 600);
    camera = new Capture(this, 160, 120);
    camera.start();
    noStroke();
}
///////////
void draw() {
    background (255);
    if (camera.available()) {
        camera.read();
    }
    // go through all the pixels in the video image
    // get the color of each pixel, and draw a circle
    for (int y=0; y<camera.height; y++) {
        for (int x=0; x<camera.width; x++) {
            color c = camera.get(x, y);
            fill (c);
            ellipse (x*spacing, y*spacing, dotSize,
            dotSize);
        }
    }
}
```

Adjust Brightness

Go to www.bloomsbury.com/richardson-data-driven, Chapter 5, and click on the project "Video Brightness."

The same color functions previously applied to a static image—red(), green(), blue(), brightness()—can also be applied to extract color information from the pixels of a moving image and used to manipulate a video image. For example, the following code can be added within the camera feed example (above) to get the brightness of each pixel color; it uses the value to set the size of each shape. The result is a distorted moving image that changes with levels of light and dark.

```
// get the color from the pixel
color c = camera.get(x, y);
fill (c); // select color for fill
float br = brightness (c); // get the brightness
value
// map brightness to usable range (0-8)
br = map (br, 255, 0, 0, 8);
// use brightness to set size of circle
ellipse (x*5, y*5, br, br);
```

An example of a pixelated "mirror" created by re-drawing the pixels from a live video source as a grid of squares.

Circles are drawn for each pixel in the video, which creates a grid-like effect. The size of each circle is adjusted according to the brightness value of the color. Light areas create smaller circles and dark areas create larger circles.

TRY IT

Re-create the example above to get and re-draw the color information from the video feed.
Modify the size of the dots and the spacing to alter the visual effect.

TRY IT

Modify the previous example you have created, and add code to get the brightness value of each pixel. Use this pixel to alter the size of each shape.

DIGITAL
SPACES

LARGE SCREEN
PROJECTIONS:
BODY
MOVEMENT

SMALL SCREEN
DISPLAYS:
DIGITAL MIRRORS

WAYS OF
SEEING

SEEING
PEOPLE

SEEING DISTANCE
AND PROXIMITY

SPOTLIGHT ON
WATSON AND
GOBEILLE

**CODE:
SEEING THE
WORLD**

NOTE: The simplest way of getting color information from a pixel in an image is by using the get() function and specifying the x, y location of the pixel to find.

```
color c = camera.get(x, y);
```

Computationally, however, a faster way is to use the pixel[] alternative, which grabs information (directly) from the pixel array.

```
color c= camera.pixel[number_of_pixel_to get];
```

The pixel array lists all the pixels in a single long list. Use the x, y location of pixel to find its position in the array by using the calculation: y*image_width+x

```
int pixelNum = y*camera.width+x;
```

```
color c = camera.pixels[pixelNum];
```

When using live video image processing, speed is more of an issue, and so using the fastest way of getting data is preferable.

Follow the Brightest Pixel

Go to www.bloomsbury.com/richardson-data-driven, Chapter 5, and click on the project "Find the Brightest Pixel."

Extracting color data from the pixels in a live image provides the ability to do useful things such as find and track specific areas of color or brightness. By comparing the values of every pixel in an image, the overall brightest, reddest, bluest, or greenest pixel can be found. This opens up creative possibilities for the creation of interactive pieces of work. For example, getting the brightest pixel in a scene can be the first step in creating interactive graphics that follow the movement of a flashlight.

To get the brightest pixel from a scene, a variable is needed to store the overall brightest pixel value. It starts with a low value, and is used to save the highest brightness value it finds:

```
float overallBrightest = 0;
```

In the nested "for" loops, the brightness value of each pixel color is found in turn and compared to the overallBrightest value. If a pixel is found with a brightness greater than the current highest level, then it is saved as the new overallBrightest value, and its location (x, y) is saved (as brightestX, brightestY). The result of this process is that for every frame in the video feed, the overall brightest pixel and its x, y location is found. A shape can then be drawn at the brightest x, y location; the following is an extract from the code that would be used to find the brightest pixel in an image.

```
float overallBrightest = 0;
//
for (int y=0; y<camera.height; y++) {
  for (int x=0; x<camera.width; x++) {
     // get the COLOR of the current pixel
     color c = camera.get(x, y);
     // get the BRIGHTNESS of current pixel
     float currentBrightness = brightness (c);
     // compare this pixel with the BRIGHTEST found
so far
     // if the current pixel is brighter than the
overall brightest,
     // then save it and its location
     if (currentBrightness > overallBrightest) {
        overallBrightest = currentBrightness;
        brightestX = x;
        brightestY = y;
     }
  }
}
// draw circle at the brightest spot
ellipse (brightestX, brightestY, 50, 50);
```

In this example, a circle shape will continually track the movement of bright lights or objects (e.g., it can track the movement of a user waving a flashlight or LED light). By extracting amounts of red, green, or blue, the same approach can be used to track spots of a specific color (e.g., to track and follow the movement of chosen lights).

An example of brightness tracking. A red circle is drawn at the location of the brightest pixel in the image. A flashlight can be used to control the movement of the shape on screen.

TRY IT

Take a look at the brightest pixel example online.
Try to re-create your own version of it.
Modify it so that the shape follows the darkest pixel or the pixel with the most amount of red.

Green Screening

Go to www.bloomsbury.com/richardson-data-driven, Chapter 5, and click on the project "Green Screen."

Extracting color information can also be used as the basis of green screening techniques, in which colors close to a particular ("key") color (e.g., bright green) are ignored (not drawn in the scene), which allows other background images or graphics to show through.

To find how close a pixel is to a specific key color, it is necessary to get the red, green, and blue values for each color and calculate the overall "distance" between them:

First the values of the amounts of red, green, and blue of the "key" color are found and saved—in this case, a brightest green:

```
color chromaKey = color (0, 255, 0);
float chromaR = red (chromaKey);
float chromaG = green(chromaKey);
float chromaB = blue (chromaKey);
```

Next, the color of each pixel in the video feed is found within the "for" loop structure and the RGB values are extracted in turn:

```
color c = camera.get(x, y);
fill (c);
// extract RGB values from the current pixel
float r = red(c);
float g = green(c);
float b = blue (c);
```

Then the "distance" between the color values is found. The dist() function returns a single number, which is the overall difference between the two sets of numbers (in this case, the RGB values); thus, it finds the "distance" between the two colors (i.e., how closely they are matched).

```
float colorDiff = dist (r, g, b, chromaR, chromaG,
chromaB);
```

DIGITAL
SPACES

LARGE SCREEN
PROJECTIONS:
BODY
MOVEMENT

SMALL SCREEN
DISPLAYS:
DIGITAL MIRRORS

WAYS OF
SEEING

SEEING
PEOPLE

SEEING DISTANCE
AND PROXIMITY

SPOTLIGHT ON
WATSON AND
GOBEILLE

**CODE:
SEEING THE
WORLD**

Colors that have small "distance" between them indicate that the "key" color and the pixel color are closely matched. Colors that most closely match the "key" green color are ignored. Only colors with a wide distance between them are drawn:

```
if (colurDiff > 180) {
    rect (x, y, 1, 1);
}
```

The overall effect in this example is that the greenest pixels are ignored; they are not drawn. Any background image or color will therefore be able to show through these gaps. In this way, a "green screen" effect can be achieved, and a figure can be made to appear in a new scene.

A simple example of a "green screen" effect. The bright green pixels from the image are ignored, allowing the background image to show through. A green piece of paper transforms in front of the camera into sky and clouds.

TRY IT

Take a look at the green screen example online.
Try to re-create your own version of it.
Modify it to alter the "key" color. Adjust the values that set the "tolerance" level of the effect.

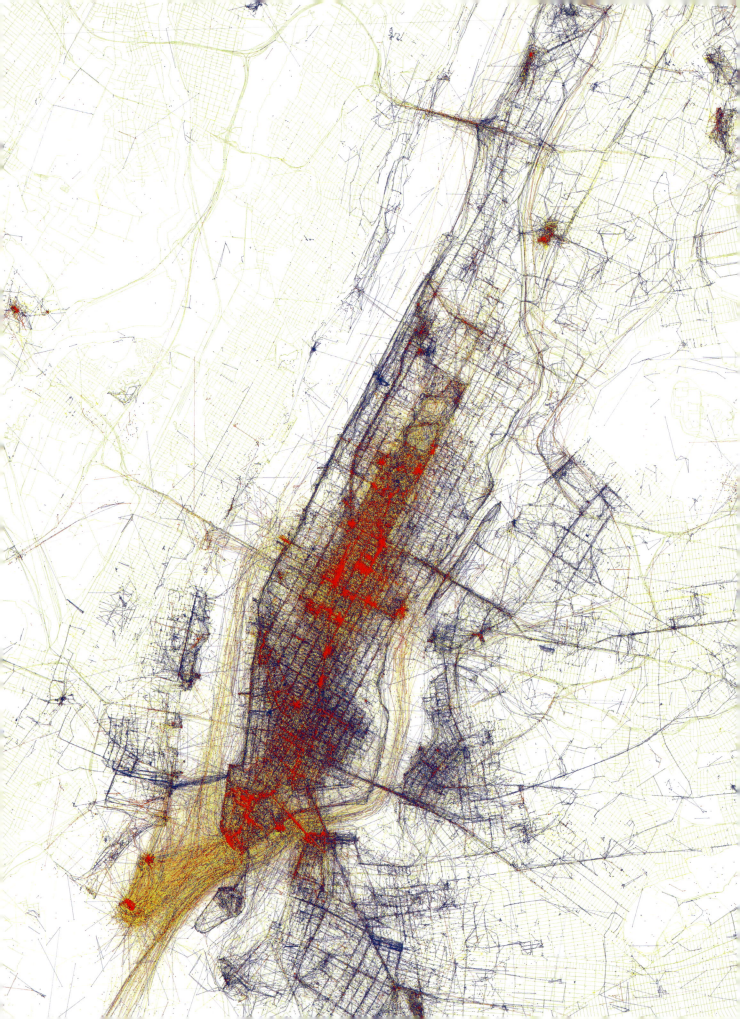

CHAPTER SIX
LARGE AND LIVE EXTERNAL DATA

**"Data visualization is all about melding
the visual and the conceptual."**
David McCandless

THE DATA-LIVED LIFE

We live in a digitally connected, data-driven world. Sophisticated mobile technology allows people to connect with each other and to data like never before. Satellite navigation systems (GPS) link us to maps and live traffic information; running watches record and share individual exercise patterns, including movement, speed, and routes taken; text and photographs can be uploaded and shared from remote locations across the globe. From government statistics via global institutions right down to individual social media messages and images, data is shared on a minute-by-minute basis, adding to a vast expanding pool of information. Our "information society" is swimming in data; it is everything and everywhere.

The term "data" can sound cold and dry, conjuring up ideas of impenetrable lists of numbers and facts; however, although it is often digitally sourced, data is *human-centered*. Each set of data represents a record of the patterns and stories of human activity. Behind every text or number list lies a story, experience, feeling, or interaction. Digital data can provide a "snapshot" of the mood or activity of a group of people during a particular time or at a specific location. It is a valuable record of narratives, emotions, ideas, and experiences.

Taking and visualizing data in a graphical format is an important and powerful way of relating the ideas, experiences, and stories of human interaction that may otherwise go untold or unseen. Complex or hard-to-digest information can be given new life and meaning by a visual image that communicates facts and information in a direct and accessible manner.

The practice of presenting data in a visual format, sometimes referred to as "information graphics," has long been a key part of graphic design and still remains a powerful and important means of visually presenting figures, facts, stories, and ideas. Charts, diagrams, and graphics have been used throughout design history to condense and communicate information in vital and meaningful way. As far back as 1858, Florence Nightingale used the now-familiar pie chart as a visual way to summarize army death rates and data highlighting how poor hygiene in hospitals caused preventable diseases. Her graphic representation of pages of hospital data brought her cause to light by condensing the facts into a single, direct piece of visual information, which helped changed the conditions in which injured soldiers were treated.

Many fields, from sports to government, use information graphics to present and communicate information for varied reasons and in diverse contexts. Information graphics can even be used to make data look beautiful. Representing data in a visual format can make content arresting and compelling for the viewer. "Beautifying" data is an important means of getting data noticed or seen in a new way. Visual design is a powerful tool for revealing hidden patterns within data and communicating them in meaningful and striking ways. The creative skills of the graphic designer therefore play an important part in communicating the "story" of data.

CODE AS A DATA VISUALIZATION TOOL

Although data visualization and information graphics have long been used as part of graphic design practice, the unprecedented rise of, and access to, digital data over the past few years has seen this area of design quickly rise to prominence as data becomes available in larger and larger quantities. In the modern data era, the most powerful tool for accessing and visualizing large data sets is not traditional graphics and drawing software tools but programming and code.

Code is a powerful data visualization environment, which creates a direct link between the data source and graphical output. Code gives designers and programmers a unique way to extract huge amounts of digital information and directly apply it to a visual output. Live data values can directly change the variables hard-wired in a piece of code that define the visuals of a digital graphic or drawing (e.g., sizes, colors, shapes, positions, etc.). Designers and programmers use code to connect external data sources to graphics and visuals in a dynamic and responsive way.

The sheer scale of the data that can be processed in this way gives designers the chance to use and represent large sets of data in increasingly complex ways. The processing power of digital programming processes allows designers the chance to create data visuals on a scale previously unimaginable. Code can sift through and organize huge amounts of data in ways manual processes cannot; it can make visual associations among the qualities found within the data values, revealing fascinating patterns of group human activity.

THE DATA-
LIVED LIFE

**CODE AS
A DATA
VISUALIZATION
TOOL**

DATA
SOURCES

MAPPING
DATA

MAPPING
SOCIETY

SPOTLIGHT ON
JER THORP

CODE:
GETTING AND
USING EXTERNAL
DATA

6.2

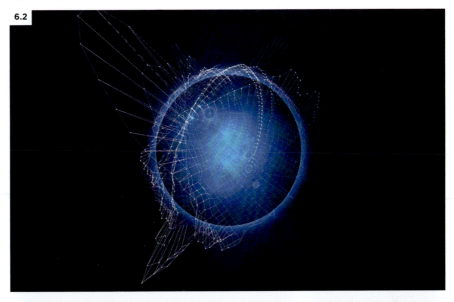

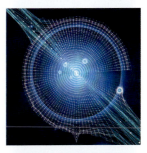

6.2 *Grid* **Futura Epsis 1**
Code can be used to visualize data from an audio source. This is an interactive multi-touch sound visualization created for live events that translates the audio track into a graphical 3D space. The application consists of a desktop version (created using Processing) for real-time graphic visualization of music and also an iOS version for interacting with the Processing app (created using openFrameworks).

DATA SOURCES

Finding and selecting the most appropriate and most interesting data source is an important part of any data visualization process. The online world is awash with data—stocks and shares, temperatures, news headlines, images, opinions, geo-locations, and so on—each of which can make a potentially interesting starting point for creative work. Data can exist as a single, live, varying value (e.g., weather information or stocks and shares values) on a website or as large, downloadable spreadsheets (e.g., Excel documents or Google docs) of statistical information gathered by governments or institutions. In an environment swimming in so much digital information, the problem often is not the lack of data but the amount of it.

Whatever the source of the data, much of the initial programming work with data values involves sifting and searching through a source to find the most useful or interesting elements of information and extracting it in a "clean" and useable format. This can mean removing erroneous, unwanted tags and text from an HTML file or sorting through rows and columns on a table of information. The process of hunting for data values is sometimes referred to as "data mining."

The following provides a summary of some of the main formats for accessing online data.

HTML

A simple way of getting at data is to directly access information from a web source. HTML (HyperText Markup Language) documents provide a good starting point for doing this. Lots of data values exist as dynamically updated elements within the body of a dynamically updated web (HTML) page. Changeable information, such as sports scores and stock values can be found within the HTML source of web documents, providing a simple, direct source of numeric data. Those individual data values can be extracted from a web page and used to drive dynamic graphics.

The source code of an HTML document can be imported directly into a program, which then sorts and sifts it, extracting useful bits of information. Once extracted, the data values from the website can be used as part of a simple but dynamic graphic. The source (HTML formatted text) of a weather forecast website may, for example, contain within the body of the page values that relate to the current and future temperature of a given city. Loading the HTML, and then sifting and extracting these values, can generate graphics that adjust with the changing weather conditions—perhaps those experienced on the other side of the world.

Although an accessible source of data, HTML formatted content does not serve the information up in an immediately accessible way; it requires the programmer to do a lot of sorting and hunting (mining) before an individual piece of data can be extracted and used.

XML

Information buried deep within the body of a web (HTML formatted) document can be read by humans, who are able, after some searching, to see and pick out the necessary data. By looking carefully through the source code, we may be able to spot values that correspond to the specific pieces of information we want. Our own ability sift through complex HTML tags to find a particular key piece of data from an HTML document is not, however, easily translatable into a computer program. Writing a code to perform the equivalent task of digging a data item out of an HTML document can become cumbersome and problematic. XML (Extensible Markup Language) documents, on the other hand, provide a more useful and accessible way of organizing data, which helps to ease this problem.

XML is a widely used formatting language for describing data in a useful and easily accessible format. Although HTML is used to describe the *content* of a page, XML is a useful way of describing the *data* within a page and provides an efficient means of getting at the nuts and bolts of data online. XML does not "do" anything; it is a tool for carrying information and an ideal format for accessing and finding information. Rather than using pre-defined tags (as in HTML), data elements in an XML file are wrapped in tags defined by the programmer, giving each item of data an accurate and easily understandable description. XML is a highly flexible format for describing data. It is used for a wide range of purposes (page content, databases, catalogues, etc.). It is a great format for grabbing and using interesting data sources.

Tabular data

API (Application programming interface)

Data in an XML document are usually nested (i.e., stored inside one another), creating a branching structure of "items" and "sub items" (equivalent to folders and sub folders). This organized, nested structure helps define and collate information in a logical and accessible manner. It allows the programmers a relatively straightforward way of digging and navigating through what could be a potentially complex set of data. Computers read XML documents much more easily than HTML documents. Code can be written to search for data details, easily navigating through the organized directory style of the XML document.

XML data is all over the web. Online data as a weather or news feed in this format can be identified, selected, and imported into programming applications that are free to represent it in new and original ways.

See Code section: XML Data (page 186).

Large quantities of national and global statistical data are collated, stored, and made available for public use from several online sources (e.g., Guardian data blog: www.theguardian.com/data). This data contains interesting facts and background figures relating to health, economies, social issues, and other areas. This type of data is typically formatted as a single large spreadsheet or table of values and properties. Information of this kind is typically exported and reformatted as a single large list of values separated either by commas or by tabs. Unsurprisingly, these are referred to as Comma Separated Values (CSV) or Tab Separated Values (TSV).

Huge lists of TSV or CSV data, although too unwieldy to be read by humans, are in a useful and easily digestible format for computer languages and programs to use. The systematic format (comma separation) of data, which removes all unnecessary text formatting, presents the "raw" data in a single simple serving, leaving programmers the relatively straightforward task of finding and extracting individual pieces of information. The CSV format is especially useful for number data on a large scale—from temperatures across the globe to trends in world health to maps of information from GPS routes and co-ordinates.

See Code sections: Comma-separated Data and Loading Table Data (page 182).

An API or "application programming interface" enables applications to communicate with one another. APIs are a good way of extracting online content in a useful format (e.g., either as XML or JSON formatted content) and are especially useful for sourcing information created online by social media applications. There are many APIs available that allow programmers and developers to access the data within their application. Both Facebook and Twitter, for example, have their own APIs, which allow developers and coders ways of extracting and accessing the comments, images, status updates, and other elements in a format that can be used to create new applications (with Processing, for instance) or data visualizations. Each API has its own reference guide and documentation, which is usually available from the content provider's "developer" section of their website (e.g., https://dev.twitter.com).

MAPPING DATA

Maps are graphical representations and interpretations of the physical world. Designers of a map present a particular, edited version of geographical landscape, adding or leaving out visible landmarks, places, and points of interest as appropriate to the map's function and purpose. In addition to the visible features of the physical world, an extra layer of data exists that can be connected to specific locations and places across the globe. Increasing amounts of data linked with locations— either via individual, location-based GPS devices or via national and international statistical data—is now available for creating visually informative, data-driven maps. A traditional map marks the physical sites and characteristics of a location; a data map marks and locates the invisible information involving human movement, experience, and interaction.

See Code section: Simple Data Map (page 185).

Mapping people

Location data pervades our digital lives. Devices that plot users' positions are increasingly commonplace. GPS (satellite) technology embedded into phones, computers, and wearable devices situate the user with a remarkable degree of accuracy. Social media applications can use and send location information, allowing people to share both the "what" and the "where" of their digital lives.

As well as being a navigation tool, location data generates a digital data trail of our lives. Data records of the locations and movements of people as they interact generate a fluid digital layer of information that programmers can communicate in data maps.

Collating large amounts of data creates a huge data cloud of thoughts and experiences—a digitally fluid map of user experience and human activity. Social media location data linked with other—informal or formal—information reveals a digital data trail of shared words, places, images, and thoughts that can be picked up by artists / designers / programmers to be visually re-interpreted to create patterns of the digital human life. These maps create a global view of individual activity, which collectively creates a new and revealing perspective on human activity.

EXEMPLAR

Onformative: 4010 Facebook tree

Deutsche Telekom commissioned onformative to design and create the Gallery Wall of their flagship store in Berlin. The store communicated with customers on Facebook, posting photos, special offers, and events. The design team printed a data visualization to cover the wall, generating it from the store's own Facebook messages and communications.

Using the Facebook Graph-API, the design team accessed and analyzed data recorded over a four-year period with a piece of custom software written in Processing. The challenge was to take the vast quantity of different data elements from the Facebook API (e.g., posts, number of likes, topics, comments, and times) and illustrate them in a single compelling data graphic.

An organic plant structure proved to be a useful visual metaphor for connecting and illustrating the different strands and elements of the social network. Leaves are generated according to the found "characteristics" of each post—for example, the creation date and time, the number of comments and likes an individual post received, as well as the topic of the post. Values from each of these elements were mapped to create the individual characteristics, shape, and color of each leaf. The amount of "red" in a leaf, for example, is determined by the number of likes a post received, and the time a post was created defines how much the leaf opens up (posts created during early morning or evening open up

THE DATA-
LIVED LIFE

CODE AS
A DATA
VISUALIZATION
TOOL

DATA
SOURCES

**MAPPING
DATA**

MAPPING
SOCIETY

SPOTLIGHT ON
JER THORP

CODE:
GETTING AND
USING EXTERNAL
DATA

less than those created during the day).
Buds spawned around the leaves reflect
the number of comments around the
post. Each type of post—whether a
message, a link, or a photo—generates
its own style of leaf with identifiable
visual characteristics. Branches are
used to connect posts according to the
date of their creation, allowing the
viewer to read the development of the
Facebook communication over time,
from the root of the tree to its top.

To generate the final layout, the team
used Processing to auto-generate
different variations and then manually
edited to get the desired layout and
look. The final result is both visually
striking and compelling in its detailed
treatment of the data. Seeing group
communication as organic form
creates a strong final visual image
that resonates with the social media
community.

6.3 *4010 Facebook Tree*
onformative design
Visualization of customers'
Facebook activity for Deutsche
Telekom, Berlin. Each branch
and fern relates to specific
themes, topics, and posts
taken from the company's own
Facebook page. The organic
structure highlights threads of
online conversation and activity
as a decorative piece of data-
driven wallpaper.

EXEMPLAR

Eric Fischer: See Something Say Something; Tourists and Locals

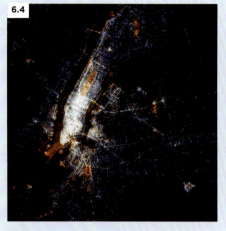

6.4

Eric Fischer is a data visualization artist / designer who uses social media information to plot maps of people's locations as they move through and around cities. The results are a series of visually stunning data maps.

Fischer uses programming code (usually C) to grab geo-located data from social media networks—notably Twitter API or Flickr. He then re-uses the information to plot pixels that reveal the locations of users as they move through a space and connect with the social network. The results of the project are shared online and create highly detailed data maps that present a new and compelling vision of our world. Towns, cities, and even countries are mapped in this way, bringing to life patterns of social media activity mapped to specific geo-locations.

A couple of notable projects from this ongoing series of experiments include "See Something Say Something" and "Tourists and Locals." In each of these experiments, Fischer explores differences in the data to differentiate and locate among types of user activity.

The "See Something Say Something" project uses color to indicate users who see something (share a photo), those who say something (Tweet some text), and those who do both. Different colored dots are mapped to indicate the locations of each of these groups.

In the "Tourists and Locals" project, color is used to indicate users who are new to the city and those who are visiting. This differentiation is gleaned by looking at the history of each user's location to determine if they have recently traveled in to town. Colors across the map reveal the limitations of tourist explorations around a city, highlighting the hot spots and boundaries of their wanderings.

Visually marking and exploring these simple differentiations in the user data adds to the way in which we understand it and adds to its visual strength.

6.4 *See Something Say Something* **Eric Fischer**
Data visualizations of New York, London, and Tokyo, created from geo-tagged Tweets of users. The colored dots indicate where a person has shared a Flikr photo (orange), or posted a Tweet (blue), or both (white).

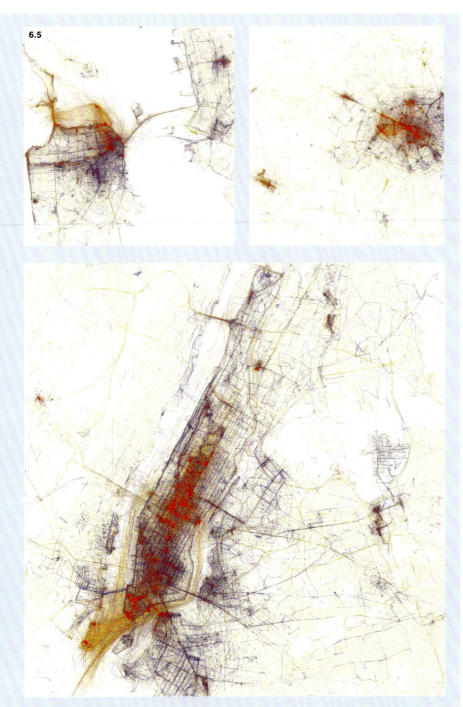

6.5

**6.5 *Tourists and Locals*
Eric Fischer**
Data visualizations of maps of New York, Paris, and San Francisco, indicating the activity of locals and visitors to the city. Blue points indicate pictures taken by locals; red points are pictures taken by tourists; yellow points are pictures of users who may be either.

Mapping journeys

As well as being able to locate and map individual user locations, data can be accessed from GPS devices, such as running watches, which record and store data of individual routes or journeys. Using this technology, individuals can map and share their own personal running or walking routes, saving and sharing each step as they journey across the landscape. A collated list of GPS (longitude and latitude) values from a run or walk provides a wealth of interesting useable number information, which can be translated into digital graphics or drawings.

A single run or walk will generate a large list of number values: the record of each step, twist, and turn of a single user's journey. (It will include extra data, as well, such as distance, elevation speed, etc.) These values, when plugged into a drawing program, can be turned into lines and strokes, creating a graphical representation of each individual journey. This kind of human-centered data connects number values with real-life experiences and allows designers and programmers to generate exciting graphics driven by unique individual experiences.

A retail installation was created as a follow-up to this initial project, which visualized a year's worth of runs from the Nike+ website. Custom software was created that replayed tens of thousands of individual runs from across three cities (New York, London, and Tokyo). The animated visualization, based on the data of thousands of individual runners, reveals individual journeys and highlights the collective energy of urban runners in each city.

EXEMPLAR

Nike +: Paint With Your Feet

Paint With Your Feet was a project created by the design agency YesYesNo to work alongside the launch of the Nike Free Run+ 2 City Pack series. Using the GPS data captured from the Nike+ device, runners were invited to create their own individual dynamic paintings with their feet.

The data taken from runners over a two-day period was collated and imported into a piece of custom software, which used it to create graphics based on specific parameters: the speed, consistency, and unique style of each person's run.

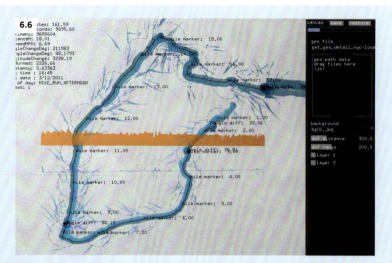

6.6 *Nike+ Paint With Your Feet*
YesYesNo
Images from the final paintings and data from each run was used to create a personalized shoe box containing a pair of the "City Pack" shoes.

THE DATA-
LIVED LIFE

CODE AS
A DATA
VISUALIZATION
TOOL

DATA
SOURCES

MAPPING
DATA

**MAPPING
SOCIETY**

SPOTLIGHT ON
JER THORP

CODE:
GETTING AND
USING EXTERNAL
DATA

MAPPING SOCIETY

Maps of data can be created from other, less personal, online sources. Archives containing vast quantities of statistical data compiled by large (social) organizations or institutions often compile and share findings and analysis of social issues, such as the health, wealth, politics, or happiness of large groups of people. Findings from this kind of data source are commonly ranked according to location (e.g., town, county, state, province, postal code, or country). Code that gives a visual value to the raw number data and maps the data according to location can therefore be used to chart social changes and attitudes across regions and countries. Finding, accessing, and visualizing this kind of information allows designers to re-present the data in a way that directly communicates issues of social and economic importance.

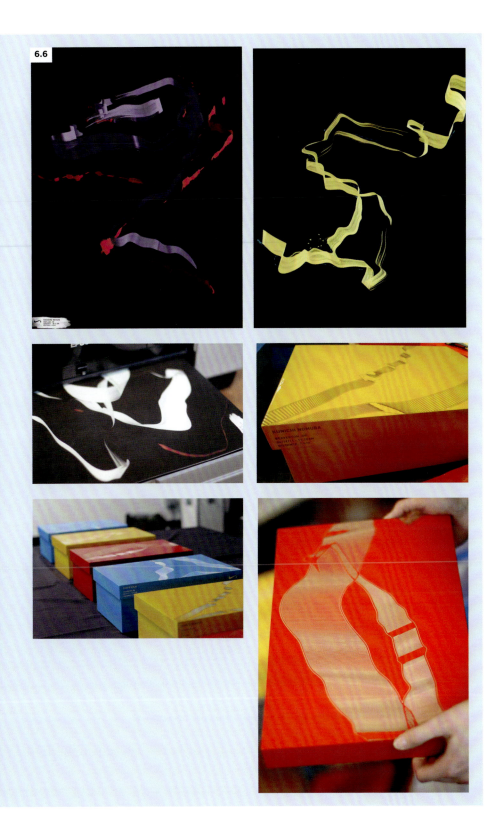

6.6

EXEMPLAR

Jed Carter: Eyes on the Sky

Eyes on the Sky is a creative investigation into generative design and the weather. Carter collected image data from sixty-four public-access webcams from across Europe (once an hour for twenty-four hours every day) and used the information to generate a set of abstract digital images. The color of the sky was extracted from each of the webcam photographs as numeric values of red, green, and blue, and Processing was used to map the color back to its correct geographic location. A final series of images, charting the changing sky colors across Europe across one week, was collated into a book of data-driven weather maps.

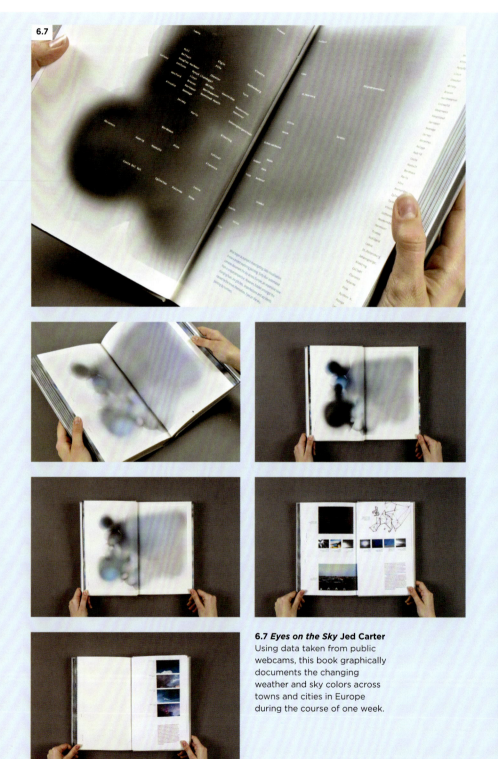

6.7

6.7 *Eyes on the Sky* Jed Carter
Using data taken from public webcams, this book graphically documents the changing weather and sky colors across towns and cities in Europe during the course of one week.

THE DATA-
LIVED LIFE

CODE AS
A DATA
VISUALIZATION
TOOL

DATA
SOURCES

MAPPING
DATA

**MAPPING
SOCIETY**

SPOTLIGHT ON
JER THORP

CODE:
GETTING AND
USING EXTERNAL
DATA

Mapping emotions

As well as being able to find and use location-based information, code can also collect and map less tangible thoughts, ideas, and feelings. The online world is like a virtual meeting-place; a public forum in which people from different social, religious, ethnic, and political backgrounds communicate personal opinions, beliefs, ideas, hopes, and fears. The digital community is alive with conversations and exchanges, ranging from the trivial to the profound, as users discuss and debate. Social media environment is a vast resource of online human emotion, charting users' communications across all parts of the globe. Tweets, status updates, images, videos, links, comments, re-posts, and blog posts all add to a vast and expanding global digital conversation.

Programming tools can dip into this vast pool of digital discussion to collect information and provide insight into the thoughts, opinions, and emotions of the online community. Code can search social media (Twitter, Facebook, blog posts) to find information about a specific theme, time, or place. Specific APIs for individual media applications give programmers access to the data behind social media activity, allowing them to search and retrieve a wide range of data, including the content of a post, embedded media, links, details of when and where a post was written, by whom, as well as links to users or associated conversations.

Searching in such a huge pool of data means that programmers need to set boundaries to prevent creating sets of results that are so large as to be meaningless. It is important to have a clear idea of the specific type of data desired; this helps give results more weight and meaning. Wide searches, using broad keywords such as "love," will produce too many results, which require further sifting and sorting. Limiting a search to a specific phrase or series of keywords gives the results more coherence and meaning. Using combinations of terms or putting parameters on the search helps. Combining phrases, such as "love" and "London," will naturally narrow down the results, offering greater insight into a particular topic.

Once results have been found, there is more work to be done to refine or categorize them to reveal hidden patterns or themes. The API of a social network application can help this refining process, allowing the programmer to dig deeper into the results. For example, looking at the time a post was written, the location, or the age of the writer gives more insight and adds more layers to the data results.

Similarly, limiting the search to a specific time frame or location can also help to clarify and filter the results. For example, searching for the word "goal" during the time of the World Cup soccer final will produce a set of results that relate to the game as it is in progress, as people comment, anticipate, or react during and after a goal is scored. Searching for the word "goal" at any other time will (naturally) produce a much broader and less interesting set of results.

Search results will always contain elements that have little or no relevance to the intended theme; however, a large enough set of meaningful results will over-ride a small number of erroneous answers.

EXEMPLAR

Jonathan Harris and Spe Kamvar: We Feel Fine

We Feel Fine is an innovative online application created by Jonathan Harris and Spe Kamvar (originally in 2005). The concept behind the work is straightforward, but the results are an extraordinary visual exploration of human emotions online.

The work continually searches a wide range of newly posted blog entries, looking for the phrase "I feel" or "I am feeling." Each time a match to either of these phrases is found, the full sentence is recorded and stored in a growing database of emotions and feelings captured from across the globe. Each entry to the database, therefore, represents a unique record of an individual's mood at a given point in time.

As well as recording the mood of a person recorded on their blog ("I feel . . ." happy, sad, etc.), the app captures other data to give a more rounded understanding of, and background for, the feeling. Data extracted from the blog, such as the age, gender, and location of the author, is saved, alongside the date and weather conditions at the time the post was written. Images from the blog post are also collated alongside the emotional sentence. Every day between fifteen and twenty thousand new feelings are added, resulting in a huge database of human feelings.

The data itself is displayed as a colorful, self-organizing particle cloud. The visual properties of each particle—its color, size, shape, and opacity—are defined according the feeling it represents. Each individual particle can be clicked on to reveal its data: the full phrase, image, and background information.

Viewing the colorful particle cloud gives an overarching picture of the kinds of emotions experienced. The particle visualization can be visually sorted and searched according to various parameters: the mood, gender, time, or location of the author. Groups of the colored particles shift or coagulate, according to the search parameters used. This means that users can discover their own graphic visualizations of human emotion. Digging deeper into the individual data combines the text and images of individual blog posts, which creates poignant and meaningful snapshots of individual experiences.

The project works as a robust and growing piece of data visualization that uses graphics to reflect moods of the online community in an engaging way. The work has been delivered as an online project and has also been produced in a book format, which adds a further layer to the design of the project.

6.8 *We Feel Fine* Jonathan Harris and Spe Kamvar
By looking for the phrase "I feel" or "I am feeling" in new blog entries, a data visualization of human emotion is created. Results can be viewed as a particle cloud of dots that can be filtered and sorted by different criteria.
Photo montages automatically combine phrases from the blog with images to create snapshots of emotions.

THE DATA-
LIVED LIFE

CODE AS
A DATA
VISUALIZATION
TOOL

DATA
SOURCES

MAPPING
DATA

**MAPPING
SOCIETY**

SPOTLIGHT ON
JER THORP

CODE:
GETTING AND
USING EXTERNAL
DATA

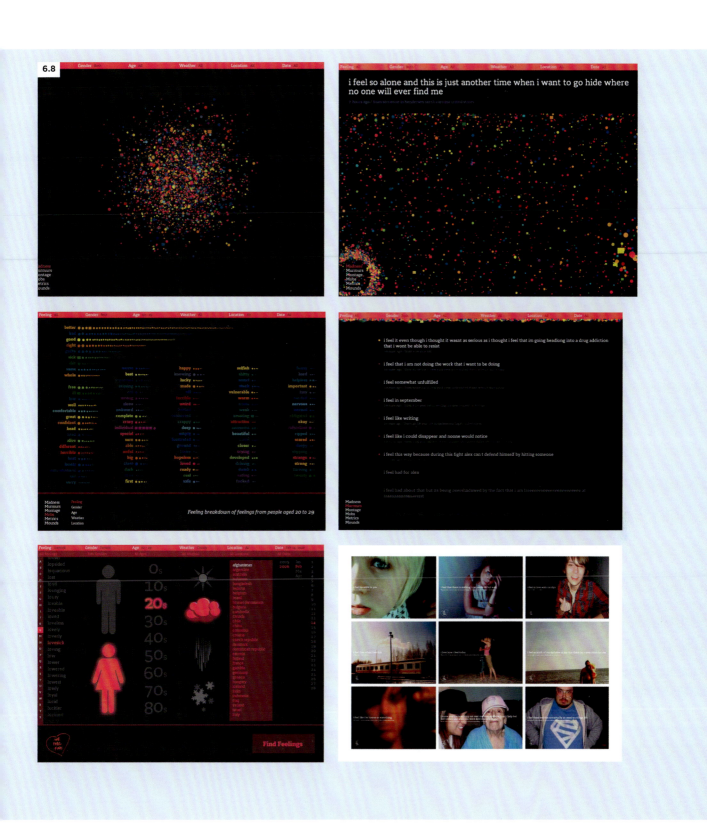

EXEMPLAR

Dario Taraborelli, Giovanni Luca Ciampaglia, and Moritz Stefaner: Notabilia

Notabilia is a research-based visualization of the discussions that take place around article deletions on Wikipedia. The Wikipedia community reviews each article posted against its "notability" guidelines to determine whether or not the topic in question is suitable for inclusion. Editors can nominate an article for deletion and, if the nomination is legitimate, a community discussion takes place, during which members discuss reasons for or against keeping it.

The Notabilia project takes the Article for Deletion discussions and visualizes the data as a series of branches in a tree-like structure. The direction and color of each branch segment is determined by individual users' views on the article as the discussion develops. Green segments leaning towards the left are created when a user recommends keeping, merging, or redirecting the article. Red segments leaning right are created each time a user recommends deleting the article.

The overall color and shape of each line is therefore a visual representation of the overall mood of the discussion as it develops. The longest one hundred discussions have been collated into a tree-like structure of branches that highlight the general flow of discussion around each topic, which is ultimately either kept or deleted.

6.9

"keep"   "delete"

THE DELETED

The 100 longest **Article for Deletion [AfD]** discussions on Wikipedia, which resulted in **deletion** of the article.

http://notabilia.net

6.9 *Notabilia* **Dario Taraborelli and Giovanni Luca Ciampaglia (data and analysis) and Moritz Stefaner (visualization)**
Organic, tree-like structures are created as visualizations of online discussions about whether or not a topic should remain or be deleted from Wikipedia. The color and direction of each branch is determined by the comments of each contributor, either for or against the subject's deletion.

THE DATA-
LIVED LIFE

CODE AS
A DATA
VISUALIZATION
TOOL

DATA
SOURCES

MAPPING
DATA

**MAPPING
SOCIETY**

SPOTLIGHT ON
JER THORP

CODE:
GETTING AND
USING EXTERNAL
DATA

6.9

THE KEPT

The 100 longest **Article for Deletion (AfD)** discussions on Wikipedia,
which did **not** result in deletion of the article (i.e. it was kept, merged or redirected).

http://notabilia.net

SPOTLIGHT ON

Jer Thorp

Jer Thorp is a generative software artist and educator whose practice explores the boundaries between science, data, art, and culture. He uses Processing code to translate large amounts of data into visual outcomes, which adds meaning and narrative, helping viewers understand and take control of the information that surrounds them.

He has worked as Data Artist in Residence at the New York Times and is an adjunct Professor in New York University's ITP program and the co-founder of the Office For Creative Research, a multi-disciplinary research group exploring new modes of engagement with data.

His visual explorations of data have produced some striking pieces of print and screen-based design. Notable examples include the 138 Years of Popular Science and Cascade projects.

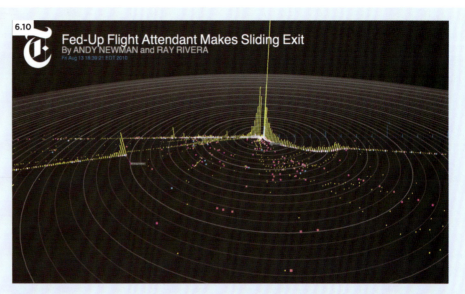

6.10

Fed-Up Flight Attendant Makes Sliding Exit
By ANDY NEWMAN and RAY RIVERA
Fri Aug 13 18:39:21 EDT 2010

Cascade

Cascade is an interactive tool created for the New York Times R&D department that visualizes how news stories and information from the organization are shared across social networks. The tool, created in Processing, gives users opportunities to explore how the more than six thousand pieces of content created each month are shared and "cascaded" across the Internet.

The application is a highly visual exploratory tool that allows a close examination into the movement of content and can be viewed either in Story mode or Cascade mode. The Story mode highlights sets of stories, which can be requested either via keyword search, section search, or using a set of "interestingness" parameters. The Cascade mode shows how an event or story cascades through the online world as it is shared and travels across social networks over a period of minutes, hours, or days.

The almost real-time based element of the application gives a unique insight into the way in which each story "unfolds" and develops over the Internet. Different 2D and 3D perspectives of the Cascade mode allow viewers to analyze the movement of conversations and information in a range of informative ways. Looking at this data in this novel, time-based way provides a valuable insight into the way in which messages are shared, capturing their movement as they spread through the ether of social media. In addition to operating as a small screen application, the Cascade project was also implemented in "exhibition" mode, staged on a five-screen video wall.

THE DATA-
LIVED LIFE

CODE AS
A DATA
VISUALIZATION
TOOL

DATA
SOURCES

MAPPING
DATA

MAPPING
SOCIETY

**SPOTLIGHT ON
JER THORP**

CODE:
GETTING AND
USING EXTERNAL
DATA

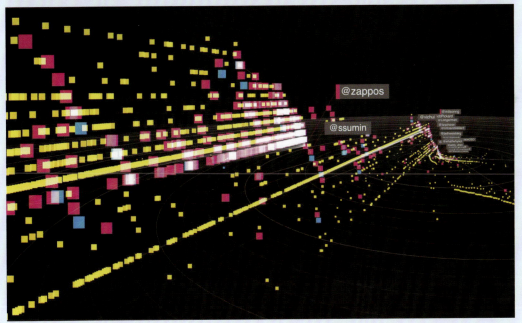

6.10 *Cascade* Jer Thorp

Cascade is an is an interactive, exploratory tool that conveys how *New York Times*' content is shared (cascades) across social networks, showing the way in which stories and ideas travel through the online world.

6.11 *138 Years of Popular Science* **Jer Thorp**
Images of a visualization piece that explores the archive of Popular Science magazine to show how different technical and cultural terms have moved in and out of use in the magazine since the start of its publication. Each year acts as an anchor connecting a range of words. Thorp used Processing as a tool to find the frequency of each word and to identify the most interesting ones to use in the final graphic.

6.11

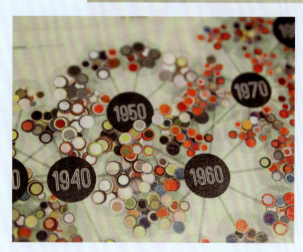

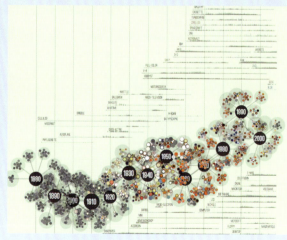

THE DATA-LIVED LIFE

CODE AS A DATA VISUALIZATION TOOL

DATA SOURCES

MAPPING DATA

MAPPING SOCIETY

SPOTLIGHT ON JER THORP

CODE: GETTING AND USING EXTERNAL DATA

Q&A: Jer Thorp

How did you develop an interest for design and programming?

I actually did some programming in BASIC when I was about ten years old, but my interest in programming really started when my Dad brought home a Mac in 1985. I learned how to program in HyperCard, which was a really amazing tool for creating simple software that combined code with visual elements. HyperCard was definitely the gateway drug for me . . . I still miss it.

Where do you look to find creative inspiration: Who or what motivates and inspires you?

I read a lot of fiction, which provides an endless supply of inspiration. I'm also very lucky to have an incredibly talented team of collaborators at The Office for Creative Research. Everyone brings something to the mix: We have architects and mathematicians and theater directors and video artists. Lately I've been spending a lot of time with Lillian Schwartz, who is a pioneer in the use of computers for art making. I've really learned a lot from her about collaboration, and about fostering cross-disciplinary thinking. She's still making art at the age of 87, which I can only dream of.

Do you think that there are specific qualities or characteristics of code that open up creative possibilities?

There's an obvious answer to that question, which is that computers + code allow us to do things which are just not possible otherwise. Here I'm thinking about iterative processes or the creation of complex forms, or the implementation of computationally difficult algorithms. I think a lot of work around computers and art has focused on these "couldn't do it before" possibilities.

I also believe that the underlying structures of code–the language itself, the syntax, the order in which it is executed–provide really rich terrain for interrogation and intervention. Artists like Casey Reas have done really profound work that investigates these possibilities.

What are the main challenges of data visualization?

The main challenge in data visualization is in restriction of choice. There are hundreds of ways in which any number or set of numbers can be mapped into visual form. Success in visualization is really about finding the mappings that are best suited to the data. Ideally you're looking for an approach that will fit the specific character of the data set and will also communicate in a way that is legible. There are a lot of unsolved problems in data visualization. Perhaps the one that interests me most is uncertainty: We really haven't yet found good ways that make sense to the public to show the potential error in data. Almost every visualization presents the data as if it was true, whereas in most cases the data is inherently inaccurate.

You have created a wide range of work, is there a particular piece or project of which you are most proud?

I am very critical of my own work: When I look back on it, I tend to see the things that are broken or erroneous or unfinished rather than the things that are supposedly successful. That said, I'm quite fond of the work that I did with Mark Hansen at the New York Times, particularly Cascade, which was a first-of-its-kind Twitter visualization tool.

Do you have any word of advice to young designers / students starting to explore data visualization for themselves?

Two things:

Sketch your ideas with a pen and paper. The clearer you are about the form your visualization will take, the easier it will be to code it. Things will change as they shift from analog to digital, but it's always a lot better to have a plan to follow rather than jumping into the code with no clear path to follow.

Start with a data set that you care about. The easiest way to satisfy this requirement is to use data about yourself: track your sleep habits for two weeks, or get your location data from your phone, or export your Gmail data. Not only will you learn about yourself, you'll also be guaranteed that you'll be working in an area where you are the expert.

CODE: GETTING AND USING EXTERNAL DATA

Loading Data from a Text File

Go to www.bloomsbury.com/richardson-data-driven, Chapter 6, and click on the project "Import Text."

There are lots of ways and lots of places from which data can come, including GPS, temperature information, and other statistics. Whatever the source, data is commonly exported into a document of text or number values that can be read into a program, sorted, and manipulated.

The simplest way of loading external data into a program is as a basic text file.

Data in a text file can be in the form of either words (Strings) or numbers, and it can be read into a file using a simple loadStrings() function and a reference to the name of the document to be loaded.

```
loadStrings ("name_of_document" );
```

(Recall that "String" is a programming term for text or information set inside inverted commas—a "string" of characters.)

The loadStrings() command reads external text data into the program and formats it as an array (a list) of individual lines. A sample text file (for example "test.txt") can be imported with the loadStrings().

```
test.txt:
I wandered lonely as a cloud
That floats on high over vales and hills,
When all at once I saw a crowd,
A host, of golden daffodils;

String lines[] = loadStrings ("test.txt");
```

The data from the text file gets automatically formatted and split into a list of individual lines. The result is an array called "lines":

```
lines [0] = "I wandered lonely as a cloud"
lines [1] = "That floats on high over vales and
hills,"
```

Getting the text as a list of lines, rather than as a single large block of text, means that the data is now in a useful and useable format of individual lines, which can be more easily sorted and output in a visual format.

Comma-separated Data

Go to www.bloomsbury.com/richardson-data-driven, Chapter 6, and click on the project "CSV Data."

As well as being used to import words, external text files can also hold and be used to import useful numerical data. Number values exported into a text file format (e.g., lists of GPS data) may be formatted as a single long list of values separated by commas and without spaces. For example:

```
Weather_data.txt:
78,82,93,85,45,44,56,78,98
```

Number values from the comma-separated document can be loaded into the program and then split and converted into a list of numbers (creating a useful set of usable values). A loadStrings() function imports the numbers as one long single string.

```
String [] loadedData = loadStrings ("Weather_data.
txt");
```

This puts the single line of numbers into the first element in an array.

```
loadedData [0] = "78,82,93,85,45,44,56,78,98"
```

The single list item, which contains all the data as one single string, can be split into an array of individual number values. The split function is a function used to split text up. In this case, it is used to split the string of numbers into a new list of

THE DATA-
LIVED LIFE

CODE AS
A DATA
VISUALIZATION
TOOL

DATA
SOURCES

MAPPING
DATA

MAPPING
SOCIETY

SPOTLIGHT ON
JER THORP

**CODE:
GETTING AND
USING EXTERNAL
DATA**

individual number values, using each comma as the cut-off point for each number (the "delimiter").

The following splits the array into an array of individual items, using the comma as the point at which to make the divisions:

```
// split the data into individual values
String[] dataAsStrings = split(loadedData[0], ',');
```

The result of this process is an array of individual numbers, written as Strings. There is a difference, in a programming environment, between a String (text) and an integer (number)—even though to us, they may look the same. For example, the String ("42") is not the same as the integer (42). The data array therefore has to be converted from Strings ("78," "82") into integers (78, 82) before they can be seen and used as numbers.

The int() function is used to convert data into number ("int") values. The entire list of data in "dataAsStrings" is converted into a new array of numbers:

```
// convert the entire array from Strings to numbers
int [] dataAsNumbers = int (dataAsStrings);
```

The result is an array of individual number values perfectly useable for creating a set of shapes or graphics.

```
dataAsNumbers [0] = 78
dataAsNumbers [1] = 82
dataAsNumbers [2] = 93
```

A "for" loop would typically be used to sort and cycle through each of the values in the array.

TRY IT

Create a text document of comma-separated numbers.
Save into the data folder of a Processing sketch, and load into the sketch using loadStrings().
Split the data into individual chunks. Create a script that draws a series of shapes based on each of the number values.

Loading Table Data

Go to www.bloomsbury.com/richardson-data-driven, Chapter 6, and click on the project "Table Data."

As well as being able to get data from a simple text file as a string of values, data can also be extracted into a program from tables of data. Data formatted into a table of columns and rows is a common way of formatting information. Spreadsheets and databases, online or offline, organize information into organized groups of columns and rows. A simple example:

```
data.tsv:
Name            Age             Gender
Andrew          42              M
Steve           36              M
Charlie         24              F
```

Data formatted in this way is a highly useful and very common way of sorting and delivering content. Information organized in this way may originate from lots of different online or offline sources (e.g., Excel or Google spreadsheets, or values generated from GPS or other types of mapping devices). Columns group information under a given topic heading (Name, Age, Gender). Rows of data are added for individual examples (Andrew, Steve, Charlie) for each group.

Information organized into a table can be exported either into a CSV (Comma Separated Values) or TSV (Tab Separated Values) format, each of which provides the raw data in a format that can be most easily grabbed and sorted by a program into rows and columns. Reading and importing values from a table allows the data to be extracted and then re-formatted.

A table from a CSV or TSV source can easily be imported by using the loadTable() function, which creates a usable grid of data from the incoming document.

```
Table table = loadTable ("data.tsv");
```

This function works in a similar way to the loadStrings() command, but instead of generating a list of String (text) information, it creates a special Table object that sorts the data into easily readable rows and columns. This provides a far easier way of working with and sorting data than would be possible if imported as a String, which would then have to be split and sorted.

Once the table is loaded, data can be extracted by looking through individual rows of information. Accessing the data means looking for specific information within rows or columns. Data in a table object is divided into a "grid" of rows and columns. Each row and column is numbered, creating a simple sort of x, y grid.

TIP: The example table above, data.tsv, has 4 rows and 3 columns. Given that the computer starts counting from zero, not one, the item in row 1, column 0, for example, is "Andrew." Row 1 is the second row in the list. Column 0 is the first column on the left.

Data from any of the individual "cells" in the table can easily be accessed by simple functions, which "get" specific types of data, using the row and column numbers as reference. The data to get will either be text, getString(), or numbers, getInt() or getFloat(). Remember, an "int" is a whole number (integer); a "float" includes decimal (floating point) numbers.

TIP: An extensive list of that which can be used when making and getting data from Tables in Processing is available online: https://processing.org/reference/Table.html

For example, the following code gets the String data (name) from the item at row 2, column 0:

```
String name = table.getString (2, 0);
println (name); // outputs "Steve"
```

Similarly, the age value (int) can be found by looking at row 2, column 1:

```
// get data from row 2 column 1
int age = table.getInt (2, 1);
println (age); // outputs "36"
```

Another way to get information from a table is to find all the data from a specific row or column using getRow() or getColumn().

For example, the following extracts an entire row of data from row 1 of the sample file:

```
// gets data first row 1
TableRow row1 = table.getRow(1);
```

Once this has been found, the items in the row (name, age, gender) can be accessed in sequence:

```
// gets the 1st item in row1 (a String)
String name = row1.getString (0);
// gets the 2nd item in the row (a number)
int age = row1.getInt (1);
// gets the 3rd item in the row (a String)
String gender = row1.getString (2);
```

These simple Processing functions are useful and efficient tools for importing, finding, extracting, and visualizing data from a large database or spreadsheet. They can be applied to a huge range of datasets and be used to create a wide range of visual purposes and outcomes.

THE DATA-LIVED LIFE

CODE AS A DATA VISUALIZATION TOOL

DATA SOURCES

MAPPING DATA

MAPPING SOCIETY

SPOTLIGHT ON JER THORP

CODE: GETTING AND USING EXTERNAL DATA

Simple Data Map

Go to www.bloomsbury.com/richardson-data-driven, Chapter 6, and click on the project "Data Map."

Using these functions, large sets of data can quickly be accessed and cycled through. For example, a larger set of data that shows the location of each state in America is saved as a "locs.tsv" file (available via the online examples). In the file, the abbreviation of each state is stored in the first column, and the corresponding grid co-ordinates of the state located in the following two columns.

```
locs.tsv:
AL      439     270
AK      94      325
.  .  .
WI      392     103
WY      207     125
```

The number values can be used as useful x, y co-ordinates to draw shapes on the screen. A "for" loop is able to do the hard work of cycling through the list of data and is used to cycle through all the rows, one at time, and for each one, get the row of data, extract the two number co-ordinates from the columns, and use them to plot a shape on the screen:

```
for (int i=0; i<table.getRowCount(); i++) {
  // get a row of data
  TableRow row = table.getRow (i);
  // get the first number value (column 1)
  int x = row.getInt(1);
  // get the second number value (column 2)
  int y = row.getInt(2);
  ellipse (x, y, 10, 10); // draw a shape
}
```

The result is a simple, but effective, data driven "map."

TIP: In this example, the "for" loop finds out how many times it has to loop (i.e., how many rows there are in the table) by using the getRowCount() function, which returns the number of rows in a table.

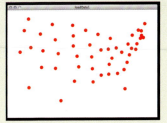

Simple example of map of state locations plotted from data from an external data file.

TRY IT

Get the "locs.tsv" data from the online examples from this chapter
Use the file as a data source to create your own visualization.
Load the data as a table.
Access the data in the rows and columns to plot shapes on the screen.

XML Data

Go to www.bloomsbury.com/richardson-data-driven, Chapter 6, and click on the project "XML Data."

XML is a useful format for reading and getting data from the web.

It is more useful and more readable for a computer program than HTML, which involves much more "mining" to extract data.

XML Structure

XML data is organized into a well-defined structure of elements and tags that can be put (nested) inside one another to create a tree (a branch-like structure).

```
clients.xml
<?xml version="1.0">
<client_list>
<person>
    <name>andrew</name>
    <age>42</age>
    <address>
        <street>main street</street>
        <town>durham</town>
    </address>
</person>
<person>
    <name>bill</name>
    <age>34</age>
    <address>
        <street>high road</street>
        <town>manchester</town>
    </address>
</person>
</client_list>
```

The top level of the document is called the "root." Elements inside the root are called "child" elements. Each element can have its own sub ("child") elements—that is, others inside of it (like a file directory) or even "parent" elements, which sit one level above.

In the example above, <client_list> is the root element of the document, into which everything sits. It has two "child" <person> elements representing different people in the <person> tags. Each <person> has its own set of child elements, which are used to store information about the name, age, and address. The parent element of <age> is the <person> element it sits within. The elements (<street> and <town>) are child elements of <address>.

This organized (root, parent, child) way of defining and organizing data makes it a simple way to create multi-layered documents that programming elements can delve into (mine) to extract data.

Loading and Accessing XML

Load XML data using the loadXML() function. This can be used to load data from a downloaded (offline) XML document, or directly to a live XML source. For example:

```
XML xml = loadXML ("clients.xml");
```

Once the XML doc is loaded, there are lots of XML-specific functions that can search and retrieve data from within the XML file. The getChild() function is a useful way to get at the data and dig (and navigate) into the structure of the document.

TIP: A full list of Processing functions for handling XML data is available online: https://www.processing.org/reference/XML.html

THE DATA-
LIVED LIFE

CODE AS
A DATA
VISUALIZATION
TOOL

DATA
SOURCES

MAPPING
DATA

MAPPING
SOCIETY

SPOTLIGHT ON
JER THORP

CODE:
GETTING AND
USING EXTERNAL
DATA

The getChild() function gets items in the document with a tag that matches the name used in the function. For example, the following will get the first "person" item in the list:

```
XML firstPerson = xml.getChild ("person");
```

A useful alternative is to grab all the "person" items as a single list, which can then be looped through and extracted for more information. The following returns a list of all the "person" items in the XML document.

```
XML [] listOfPeople = xml.getChildren ("person");
```

Having grabbed a full list of the main content, each element (person) in the list can be found and looked at to get the details of each person's name, age, and address data. This is done by taking an item in the list and using the getChild() function to grab this detail. The following example finds the XML elements "name" and "age" of the first person in the list.

```
// gets XML element called name and age from the
first person in the list
// gets <name> Andrew </name>
XML name = listOfPeople[0].getChild ("name");
XML age = listOfPeople[0].getChild ("age");
```

This process gets the XML item, including the tags (e.g., <name> Andrew </name>). The getContent() function will extract the content of the data within the tags, a much more useful format:

```
String name_data = name.getContent();
String age_data = age.getContent();
println (name_data);
println (age_data);
```

Although this is a very simple example, being able to extract and use XML data from offline or online sources is a valuable way of sourcing live data that can be used to inform graphics and visuals.

CONCLUSION

Each of the chapters throughout the course of this book has demonstrated different ways in which programming code can open up creative approaches to help designers think in new ways and create new types of digital work. It is hoped that this book has provided a greater appreciation of the role that code can play as a part of creative design practice and encouraged readers to see that computer-based design encompasses a wide vista of creative approaches and possibilities.

Seeing code as a key part of creative design practice is important. It is a way to develop a fresh approach to creating work for the data-driven environment, to re-think a default reliance on off-the-shelf software tools, and to inspire a different perspective on creative digital processes.

Having a greater understanding and appreciation of the possibilities for creating computationally driven design provides an important springboard for generating original creative concepts that harness the data input / output capability of the digital environment. It also fosters an approach to digital design that will continue to be valuable even as the technology changes.

Although not a tangible, physical, media like paint or ink, getting your "hands dirty" with code is an experimental, playful process in which imagination and creativity are crucial. This type of approach requires a broader perspective towards code that is not restricted in its limits or in its creative ambition. A narrow vision of code can be constraining, limiting programming to

a purely functional, machine-like tool, useful only for repetitive and laborious computational tasks. However, when put into the hands of creative artists, programmers, and designers, code opens up a new realm of imaginative possibilities—one that can create new, unique visual outcomes of graphics, drawings, and interactions.

The experimental, playful process of exploring code as part of digital design practice can be likened to other types of creative processes, environments, and mediums. Just as an artist explores the traditional processes and materials of paint, ink, or chalk to discover and develop his or her own visual style, so too artists and designers whose work uses the "material" of programming engage in a similar exploratory process to discover their own approach to, and way of working with, code. Like finding a personal style of drawing or painting, successfully writing code to create unique pieces of work is a matter of developing an individual approach to the types and uses of the programming functions and instructions. Although code can be easily copied and pasted to create generic-looking pieces of work, the creative "eye" of the individual designer or programmer needs to be harnessed to create work that stands above the rest. Engaging with a creative process to explore a specific element of computational data raises the work beyond the generic into something that is individual and unique. Each piece of work featured in this book is an expression of the creative vision of the individual artist or designer behind the work; it is a product of their own creative experiments and investigations, used to explore a specific aspect of coding and to create pieces of computational work that possess an individual style. Whether exploring large sets of data, making experimental computational drawings, or producing code-generated typography, each of the designers and artists featured herein have developed, through their personal practice, their own approach and way of using code to express their unique creative vision and identity.

When exploring ways to integrate the processes of code as part of creative practice, it is therefore important to develop a personal approach to explore your own ideas and vision. The range and types of code and data are so wide and varied that, like every other artist or designer, a particular area of interest or specialism needs to be developed. Whether the main interest is in graphics, drawings, or typography, each designer needs to develop a focal point, a central area of interest, around which ideas can grow develop and flourish. You may be keen to explore the capacity of code to produce large-scale generative drawings, computational letterforms, or visualizations of social media. The focal point, whatever it is, forms an important hub for creative exploration and play.

Playing with code allows ideas to emerge. Creative computational pieces grow from very simple starting points. Even the most complex piece of programming starts with a few lines that establish the broad parameters, the overall concept, of the work. By incrementally adding to and changing elements one by one, ideas develop and grow in different directions. A generic explanation or simple tutorial can be the starting point, the "seed," for a huge range of new ideas and experiments. Perhaps some, or maybe even just one, of the ideas or concepts featured in this book of "seeds" will be the starting point for a whole garden full of your own unique creative explorations into code.

APPENDIX

BIBLIOGRAPHY

Blauvelt, A. and van Mensvoort, K. (2013) *Conditional Design: Workbook*. Valiz.

Bohnacker, B., Gross, B., and Laub, J. (2012) *Generative Design: Visualize, Program, and Create with Processing*. Princeton Architectural Press.

Borenstein, G. (2012) *Making Things See: 3D vision with Kinect, Processing, Arduino, and MakerBot*. Maker Media.

Dawes, B. (2006) *Analog in, Digital Out: Brendan Dawes on Interaction Design*. New Riders.

Fry, B. (2007) *Visualizing Data: Exploring and Explaining Data with the Processing Environment*. O'Reilly Media.

Haeckel, E. (1899) *Art Forms of Nature*. Prestel (reprinted 2008).

Klanten, R. (2010) *Data Flow: v. 2: Visualizing Information in Graphic Design*. Die Gestalten Verlag.

Klanten, R. (2011) *A Touch of Code: Interactive Installations and Experiences*. Die Gestalten Verlag.

Lima, M. (2011) *Visual Complexity: Mapping Patterns of Information*. Princeton Architectural Press.

Lupton, E. (2008) *Graphic Design: The New Basics*. Princeton Architectural Press.

Maeda, J. (2000) *Maeda @ Media*. Thames & Hudson.

Maeda, J. (2004) *Creative Code: Aesthetics and Computation*. Thames & Hudson.

Pearson, M. (2011) *Generative Art*. Manning Publications.

Reas, C. (2015) *Processing: A Programming Handbook for Visual Designers and Artists*. MIT Press.

Reas C. and McWilliams C. (2010) *Form+Code in Design, Art, and Architecture*. Princeton Architectural Press.

Rendgen, S. (2012) *Information Graphics*. Benedikt Taschen Verlag.

Sauter, J., Jaschko, S., and Angesleva, J. (2011) *ART+COM: Media Spaces and Installations*. Die Gestalten Verlag.

Shiffman, D. (2008) *Learning Processing 2.0: A Beginner's Guide to Programming Images, Animation, and Interaction*. Morgan Kaufmann.

Shiffman, D. (2012) *The Nature of Code: Simulating Natural Systems with Processing*. The Nature of Code.

Thompson, D. W. (1917) *On Growth and Form*. Canto Classics (reprinted 2014).

Troika (2010) D*igital by Design: Crafting Technology for Products and Environments*. Thames and Hudson.

Yau, N. (2011) *Visualize This: The Flowing Data Guide to Design, Visualization, and Statistics*. John Wiley & Sons.

WEBOGRAPHY

Processing
https://processing.org

openProcessing
http://www.openprocessing.org

Boris Müller
http://www.esono.com

Conditional Design
http://conditionaldesign.org

Creative Applications
http://www.creativeapplications.net

Daniel Brown
http://www.danielbrowns.com

Daniel Shiffman
http://shiffman.net

design I/0
http://design-io.com

FIELD
http://www.field.io

Jer Thorp
http://blog.blprnt.com

Joshua Davis
http://www.joshuadavis.com

Moving Brands
http://www.movingbrands.com

Robert Hodgin
http://roberthodgin.com

Universal Everything
http://www.universaleverything.com

YES YES NO Interactive
http://www.yesyesno.com

PICTURE CREDITS

1.1–1.2: © Universal Everything

1.3: Courtesy FIELD and SomeOne

1.4–1.6: Courtesy John Maeda

1.7: Courtesy Processing.org

1.8: Courtesy vvvv—a multipurpose toolkit

1.9–1.10: Courtesy NodeBox

2.2: Courtesy Reza Ali

2.3: Courtesy Bartosz Hadyniak/Getty Images

2.4: Test patterns for The Puddle poster, edition 13. Designed by A. Gysin and S. Vanetti

2.5: Posters for The Puddle, edition 1 and 13, Silkscreen on colored paper, 210 x 420mm. Designed by A. Gysin and S. Vanetti, 2011–2013

2.6–2.7: Courtesy Marius Watz

2.9: Courtesy Casey Reas and the bitforms gallery, New York

2.10–2.11: Courtesy Moving Brands®

2.12: © Universal Everything

2.13: Courtesy Moving Brands®

2.14: Peter Macdiarmid/Getty Images

2.16: Courtesy Casey Reas and the bitforms gallery, New York

2.17: Courtesy Holger Lippmann

2.18: Courtesy FIELD

2.19: Courtesy Sagmeister & Walsh

2.20: Courtesy Design I/O—http://design-io.com

3.1 and 3.18: Sennep Ltd. in collaboration with Yoke

3.2: (top) Saul Landell/Mex/Getty Images (bottom) Fiona Elisabeth Exon/Getty Images

3.3: Courtesy www.BioLib.de

3.4: © ART+COM Studios, Berlin

3.5–3.6: Courtesy Moniker/conditionaldesign .org/studiomoniker.com/thursdays .studiomoniker.com

3.7: Phil Cardamone/Getty Images

3.10: Emma Johnson/Getty Images

3.11: Courtesy Robert Hodgin

3.12: Courtesy Holger Lippmann

3.15: Lightweeds, Simon Heijdens, 2005. Museum of Modern Art New York 2014/ Lightweeds, Simon Heijdens, 2005. Utah Museum of Natural History, Salt Lake City 2011

3.16: Courtesy Golan Levin. BP for StudioAKA, London and Art+COM, Berlin, Germany

3.17: Radiohead/Thom Yorke, Nigel Godrich, Stanley Donwood, Universal Everything

3.18: Sennep Ltd. In collaboration with Yoke

3.19: Courtesy Bibliothèque

3.20: Courtesy Everyware

3.21–3.22: Courtesy Daniel Brown

4.1: Courtesy Poetry 2003. Team: Petra Michel, Boris Müller, Florian Pfeffer. www.esono.com/boris/projects/poetry03/

4.2: Courtesy Kyuha Shim

4.3–4.4: Courtesy Ricard Marxer

4.5: (A) Yeohyun Ahn. Geomerative library by Ricard Marxer, Binary tree algorithm, the font, Stanford, in Processing, created by Casey Reas and Ben Fry. (G) Yeohyun Ahn. Geomerative Library by Ricard Marxer, Binary Tree. Algorithm, the font, Arial, in Processing by Casey Reas and Ben Fry. (Y) Yeohyun Ahn. Geomerative library by Ricard Marxer, Binary tree algorithm, the font, Arial, in Processing by Casey Reas and Ben Fry.

4.6: Courtesy Reza Ali

4.7: Courtesy Elena Kalaydzhieva

4.8: Concept, Design and Programming by Andreas Müller

4.9: From "Zoology." Poem by Sasha West, design by Ernesto Lavandara

4.10: From "Walking Together What Remains" by Chris Green (Interface by Erik Natzke)

4.11: Courtesy Peter Cho

4.12: Poetry 2002. Team: Friederike Lambers, Boris Müller, Florian Pfeffer. www.esono.com/boris/projects/poetry02/

4.15: Studio NAND 2010

4.16: © 2013, Vladimir V. Kuchinov

4.17–4.18: Courtesy Ariel Malka

5.1 and 5.5: Courtesy Random International

5.2: Courtesy Bede's World/Vector76/The App Chaps

5.3: Courtesy The App Chaps

5.4: Courtesy Baggar and Yoram Mesuere

5.6: Courtesy Moving Brands®

5.7: © Matthieu Savary (Smallab.org)

5.9: Courtesy Sennep Ltd

5.10: Matthew Lloyd/Stringer/Getty Images

5.12: Courtesy Hellicar&Lewis

5.15: Courtesy Robert Hodgin

5.16–5.18: Courtesy Local Projects

5.19: Design I/O—http://design-io.com

6.1 and 6.4–6.5: Courtesy Eric Fischer

6.2: © Futura Epsis 1

6.3: onformative/ Cedric Kiefer/ www.onformative.com

6.6: Designed and Produced by YesYesNo in collaboration with DualForces. YesYesNo Team: Zach Lieberman, Emily Gobeille and Theo Watson. Software made with openFrameworks. http://yesyesno.com, http://dualforces.com, http://openframeworks.cc

6.7: Courtesy Jed Carter

6.8: Courtesy Jonathan Harris and Sep Kamvar

6.9: Notabilia: Moritz Stefaner, Dario Taraborelli and Giovanni Luca Ciampaglia, 2011. http://notabilia.net/

6.10–6.11: Jer Thorp, o-c-r.org

INDEX

A

actionScript, 21
Adobe After Effects, Expressions, 21
Adobe Flash, actionScript, 21
Adobe Illustrator, 32, 33, 40, 48
Adobe Photoshop, 40, 48
Ahn, Yeohyun, 101
Ali, Reza, 33, 102
animation, 81, 124–125. *See also* movement
API (application programming interface), 165, 166, 168, 173
arguments, 22
arrays. *See* lists and arrays
Art Forms of Nature (Haeckel), 66, 67
ART+COM, 68–69
audio. *See* sound
augmented reality technology, 130, 131

B

Bagger, 132
Bede's World Museum app, 131
Big Eyes Identity Illustrations (FIELD & SomeOne), 13
Biological Illustration (Haeckel), 67
BlobDetection, 140
blocks of code, 23, 93–95
Bloom (Hodgin), 73
Body Dysmorphia (Hodgin), 145–146
"boids" model, 81
books
    dynamic typography based on, 114–115, 116–117, 118–119
    reactive graphics in, 16–17
Boolean data, 25
Born magazine, 106–107
bounce, 91
Box2D for Processing, 95
brackets
    arguments in, 22
    curly, 23
    square, 28
Bridge Hypothesis (Watz), 39
brightness() function, 154, 156–158
Brown, Daniel, 84–87

C

Caligraft (Marxer), 99
Carter, Jed, 172
Casa da Musica identity (Sagmeister & Walsh), 53
Cascade (Thorp), 178–179
char data types, 120
charAt() function, 122, 123
Cho, Peter, 109
Ciampaglia, Giovanni Luca, 176–177
class programming, 93–95

Cleveland Museum of Art, 147–149
Cloud Forest-Nebelwald (Lippmann), 74
code
    animation using, 124–125
    arguments in, 22
    blocks of, 23, 93–95
    bounce using, 91
    brightness() function in, 154, 156–158
    charAt() function in, 122, 123
    class programming using, 93–95
    code libraries for, 95, 140, 144, 155
    color using, 120, 152–159
    comments in, 23
    computer vision libraries for, 140
    creativity and, 12–13, 188–189
    as data visualization tool, 162–163
    decision making in, 25–29
    designers using (*see* designers)
    digital environments via, 88–95
    dist() function in, 158
    draw() function in, 28, 40
    drawing with numbers via, 32–33, 44, 46, 48, 52, 53, 56–63
    drawLetter() function in, 125
    dynamic typography using, 98, 99, 100, 102, 103, 104, 108, 110, 114, 120–127
    elasticity and spring using, 92
    ellipse() function in, 56–57
    environmental forces via, 89–92, 94–95
    equals() function in, 122
    external data using, 162–163, 165, 166–167, 168, 171, 173, 178, 180, 182–187
    fill() function in, 120
    float data in, 24–25, 184
    friction and damping using, 89–90
    functions in, 22–23 (*see also specific functions*)
    get() function in, 152–153, 157
    getChild() function in, 187
    getFloat() function in, 184
    getInt() function in, 184
    getRowCount() function in, 185
    getString() function in, 184
    getting started using, 18–21
    grammar and syntax, 23
    gravity using, 90, 94–95
    green screening using, 158–159
    growth and form via, 66, 68, 69, 72, 73–75, 77, 79, 88–95
    "if" statements in, 25–26, 91
    image() function in, 152–153
    importing live video sources via, 155–156
    indexOf(string) function in, 122
    int() function in, 183
    integer data in, 24, 183, 184

length() function in, 122, 123
line() function in, 56
lists and arrays in, 28–29, 95, 157, 182–183 (*see also* String data)
loadFont() function in, 121
loadImage() function in, 152–153
loadStrings() function in, 126–127, 182
loadTable() function in, 183–184
loadXML() function in, 186
loops in, 26, 28, 29, 40, 59–60, 61, 69, 73, 90, 95, 123, 153, 155, 157, 183, 185
loops in the structure in, 28
manipulating medium via, 12–13
map() function in, 154
mathematical symbols in, 24, 25–26
moveLetter() function in, 125
object oriented programming using, 78, 93–95, 124–125
PFont class in, 121
PImage class in, 152–153
pixel[] alternative in, 157
point() function in, 56
popMatrix() function in, 62
programming languages in, 12, 15, 18–21, 22, 164–165 (*see also* processing)
pushMatrix() function in, 62
radians() function in, 63, 88
random() function in, 60–61
rect() function in, 56–57
red(), green(), blue() functions in, 154, 158–159
repetition in, 40, 59–60, 61, 69, 72, 73–75 (*see also* loops)
rotate function in, 62–63
seeing the world using, 134, 138, 140, 144, 147, 152–159
setup() function in, 28
sine waves in, 72, 88–89
split() function in, 122, 126
splitTokens() function in, 126
String data in, 25, 120, 121–122, 123–124, 126–127, 182–183, 184
subString() function in, 122
text() function in, 120, 123
text in, 110, 114, 120–124, 126–127, 182
textFont() function in, 121
textSize() function in, 120
textWidth() function in, 124
translate() function in, 62–63
triangle() function in, 56
user-defined functions in, 27
variable data types in, 24–25 (*see also* float data; integer data; String data)
variables in, 23–25, 52, 58–59, 69, 93, 121–122
video library for, 155

ACKNOWLEDGMENTS

I would like to express my sincere thanks to all those who generously contributed their work, without which this book would not have been possible. I would also like to thank all those who helped with the writing and editing process by offering comments, advice, and encouragement.

Special thanks go to my wife, Loraine, and son, James, for their constant support and patience.

The publishers would like to thank Gavin Allanwood, Jamie Steane, Michael Salmond, Joseph Reinsel, Joel Swanson, and Wayne Madsen.